Compan
Revised Comm

10. Praying with the Scriptures

Already published

Companion to the Revised Common Lectionary

1: Intercessions

2: All Age Worship Year A

3: All Age Worship Year B

4: All Age Worship Year C

5: Before We Worship

6: Mining the Meaning Year A

7: Mining the Meaning Year B

8: Mining the Meaning Year C

9: Dramatic Dialogues

Neil Dixon

Companion to the Revised Common Lectionary

10. Praying with the Scriptures

EPWORTH PRESS

British Library Cataloguing in Publication data

A catalogue record for this book is available
from the British Library

0 7162 0576 9

First published in 2004
by Epworth Press
4 John Wesley Road
Werrington
Peterborough PE4 6ZP

Printed and bound in Great Britain by
Biddles Ltd, www.biddles.co.uk

This book is dedicated
to the memory of
A. Raymond George,
Ronald Lawton
and
Gwynneth M. Spoors.

Contents

Preface

More than twenty years have passed since the publication of *Companion to the Lectionary, Volume 3: A New Collection of Prayers*, which I edited for the Epworth Press. In the preparation of that volume, I was joined by eighteen other contributors, which meant that there was considerable variety in the style and content of the prayers. I am grateful to have the opportunity now to contribute to the new series of *Companions to the Revised Common Lectionary*, but this time I have worked alone.

Most of the prayers in this book are new, though that statement requires qualification in several respects. First, I have included revised versions of some of the prayers that I myself wrote for *Companion to the Lectionary, Volume 3*. Second, as a tribute to their memory, I have incorporated amended versions of a number of prayers originally written by three contributors to the earlier volume who have died since its publication, and to whom this book is dedicated. Third, I have quite deliberately drawn on the language and imagery which the Bible readings and Psalms set for each occasion in the *Revised Common Lectionary* supply, using *The New Revised Standard Version of the Bible (Anglicized Edition)* for this purpose. Biblical images from all three lectionary years will usually be found in each set of prayers. Fourth, I have consciously (and probably sometimes unconsciously) borrowed phrases from the rich tradition of hymnody; and sixteen prayers are directly based on verses from hymns, especially hymns by Charles Wesley.

I am grateful to the Revd Gerald Burt, who was Editorial Secretary to the Epworth Press at the time when this book was first commissioned and also when it was completed, for his patience and encouragement. As always, my wife, Julie, and my children, Thomas and Emily, have been immensely supportive.

Neil Dixon
March 2003

Introduction

The contents of this book are offered for use in public worship, alongside the provisions of the *Revised Common Lectionary*, as used in *The Methodist Worship Book*. It is assumed that the services in which they are used will normally be structured as recommended in the *Morning, Afternoon, or Evening Services* which are included in *The Methodist Worship Book*: that is, they will have a fourfold structure of Preparation, Ministry of the Word, Response and Dismissal.

An opening sentence is provided for each Sunday or other occasion. This sentence is almost always drawn from the readings or psalms for that day in one of the three lectionary years, though during the Easter season and on one or two other occasions this is not the case. It is good to begin an act of worship with appropriate words from Scripture.

Four prayers are then supplied for each occasion. The first is a prayer of adoration and/or approach. The second is a prayer of confession. It is intended that these two prayers should be used in the first part of the service, the Preparation, though, as *The Methodist Worship Book* suggests, there may be occasions when confession appropriately follows the Ministry of the Word.

The third prayer is one of thanksgiving, and the fourth is a prayer of dedication. These prayers should normally be used in the Response.

Conspicuously absent from this volume are prayers of intercession. The omission is not because such prayers are deemed unimportant: they are, of course, a vital component of public prayer. But there are many available sources of, and suggestions for, intercessory prayer, and Christine Odell's collection in the present series (Volume 1. Intercessions) is a fine example.

Approach and Adoration

In about half the opening prayers, the elements of approach to God and adoration are combined. In the others, only one of these elements appears. Approach to God or adoration may well have been expressed in the first hymn of the service, and this is especially desirable when one of these elements is absent from the prayer supplied.

Confession

The Christian gospel not only makes us conscious of our sinfulness; it also assures us of God's love and compassion. For this reason, prayers of confession should also contain, or be followed by, the assurance of forgiveness. In a few cases, the prayers of confession in this book are followed by a formal declaration of forgiveness, but for the most part, the conviction that God is merciful and forgives the sins of those who repent is built into the prayers themselves. Those who prefer to make a definite statement of absolution on every occasion could, of course, use one of the examples which appear in this book, for instance on page 9, or in many places in *The Methodist Worship Book.*

For the sake of completeness, prayers of confession are provided for each occasion, although there is much to be said for the omission of confession on Christmas Day, Easter Day and Pentecost, when the note of exuberant joy should be dominant in an act of worship.

Thanksgiving

The prayers of thanksgiving are designed to be wide-ranging, celebrating the whole sweep of 'salvation history', however briefly, on every occasion, and thus echoing the traditional eucharistic prayer. It may sometimes be appropriate for specific thanksgivings to be inserted into these prayers, which provide a framework in which the mighty acts of God in creation and redemption are recalled.

Dedication

A number of the prayers of dedication are written on the assumption that they will be used immediately after the Offering, but in every case the principal theme is the dedication of the worshippers' lives to God.

Responses

In some of the prayers, a congregational response has been included. Each of these has been kept short and succinct (and thus easily remembered by the congregation). Users who wish to make some of the other prayers responsive can, of course, do so by splitting them up at appropriate points and inserting a suitable versicle and response.

Although this book has been written by a Methodist, with the requirements of the Methodist 'preaching service' very much in mind, it is hoped that its contents will be useful to leaders of worship and congregations, both Methodist and non-Methodist.

PRAYERS

FIRST SUNDAY OF ADVENT

Opening Sentences

Night is far gone and the day is at hand. The Son of Man will come with power and great glory.

Prayer of Approach and Adoration

Great God of wonders,
you reign supreme over all.
You meet those who gladly do right,
who remember you in their ways;
and in your abundant mercy
you do not remember our sins for ever
but call us into the fellowship of your Son.
We come into your house,
rejoicing in your steadfast love,
and we praise your holy name;
through Jesus Christ our Lord. **Amen.**

Prayer of Confession

Merciful God,
as we wait for the revealing of our Lord Jesus Christ,
we confess that we are sinners.
You call us to live as children of the light,
but we have sought to hide away in darkness.
You set before us a glorious hope,
but we wallow in despair.
Forgive us, O God;
be mindful of your mercy.
Make us to know your ways;
teach us your paths;
lead us in your truth;
and strengthen us by your Spirit;
for you are the God of our salvation,
made known in Jesus Christ our Lord,
in whose name we pray. **Amen.**

Prayer of Thanksgiving

Eternal God,
we give you thanks and praise.
In your power and love you created us;
we are all the work of your hand.
In your mercy and grace
you have sent your Son to be our Saviour.
Born of Mary,
living among us,
dying and rising,
he revealed your grace and truth.
By the power of your Spirit,
you call us to look forward in hope
to the Day that is surely coming
when Christ's glory shall be revealed.
For all your mighty acts we give you thanks and praise;
through Jesus Christ our Lord. **Amen.**

Prayer of Dedication

Faithful God,
whose promises are sure
and whose love never ends,
we offer our gifts and our lives to you.
Make us abound in love,
for you, for one another and for all,
and strengthen our hearts
that we may be blameless before you
at the coming of our Lord Jesus Christ.
We ask it for his sake. **Amen.**

SECOND SUNDAY OF ADVENT

Opening Sentence

The glory of the Lord shall be revealed and all people shall see it together.

Prayer of Adoration

Eternal God,
for you one day is like a thousand years
and a thousand years are like a day.
You are beyond time,
beyond space,
beyond our deepest thought.
Yet in your constant love
you feed your flock like a Shepherd;
you judge your people with righteousness;
and you have visited and redeemed your people
in Jesus Christ your Son.
All praise and glory belong to you,
in time and in eternity;
in Jesus Christ our Saviour. **Amen.**

Prayer of Confession

God of mercy and grace,
we confess to you what we are.
We are members of a sinful race
and each of us is a sinner.
We have wandered from your ways
and chosen our own paths.
We have ignored the message of your prophets
and trusted in our own judgement.
We have lived for the present moment
and lost sight of the hope of our calling.
Yet you are gracious and merciful;
you forgive your people and pardon all their sin.
Have mercy upon us, we pray,
and fill us with joy and peace
that we may abound in hope

by the power of the Spirit;
through Jesus Christ our Lord. **Amen.**

Prayer of Thanksgiving

Mighty God,
by your word the whole creation was formed,
and by your power and love it is upheld.
You made us, male and female,
in your image and likeness;
and, though we marred that image,
you love us still.
You have spoken to us through the prophets
and you sent your servant John
to prepare the way for the coming of your Son,
our Saviour Jesus,
who lived among us,
humble and gentle,
strong and dependable,
wise and good.
He died on the Cross for the salvation of all
and you raised him to life with power and great glory.
Through the Holy Spirit,
whom you have sent in his name,
we offer you our thanks and praise,
and long for the day when righteousness shall flourish
and peace abound
and all the earth shall know you
as fully as the waters cover the sea.
We pray in the name of Christ our Lord. **Amen.**

Prayer of Dedication

Loving God,
every good and perfect gift comes from you.
We dedicate to your service all that we have and are,
and we pray that our offering may be pleasing to you
in Jesus Christ our Lord. **Amen.**

THIRD SUNDAY OF ADVENT

Opening Sentence

The Lord God is our strength and our might and has become our salvation.

Prayer of Approach and Adoration

Mighty God,
enthroned in glory,
your being is greater than we can comprehend,
more wonderful than we can understand,
and yet you have revealed yourself to us in humility and grace.
Our spirits rejoice in you, our Saviour,
whose mercy is constant from generation to generation.
As we come into your presence
in the name of your Son
and in the power of your Spirit,
we worship and adore you.
All glory and praise be yours, now and for ever. **Amen.**

Prayer of Confession

'God has shown strength with his arm; he has scattered the proud in the thoughts of their hearts. He has brought down the powerful from their thrones and lifted up the lowly; he has filled the hungry with good things, and sent the rich away empty.'

Compassionate God,
whose Son Jesus Christ came to bring good news to the oppressed,
we confess that we too often forget the values of your kingdom.
We are proud and self-reliant;
we admire wealth and power;
we turn aside from the poor and the hungry;
we live for ourselves alone.
Forgive and renew us, we pray.
Teach us to trust in you
and to follow the example of your Son,
our Saviour Jesus Christ,
in whose name we pray. **Amen.**

Prayer of Thanksgiving

God,
who made heaven and earth, the sea, and all that is in them,
you are our strength and our might.
You made a covenant with your people
and raised up witnesses to your mighty deeds.
Despite our wilful disobedience,
you have not left us alone,
but have sent your Son to deliver us from sin and death.
When the time was right,
John appeared in the desert,
bearing witness to one mightier than himself,
the true Light that was coming into the world,
Jesus Christ our Lord.
We give you thanks and praise
for Christ's living and dying and rising,
for the good news that he brings,
and for the hope that you give us in him.
Sustain us by your Spirit
that we too may witness to Christ's glory,
for he is alive and reigns with you,
in the unity of the Holy Spirit,
one God, for ever and ever. **Amen.**

Prayer of Dedication

Eternal God,
to whom we owe our very being,
we bring to you our gifts and our lives.
Receive what we offer as tokens of our gratitude
and signs of our dedication of our lives to your service;
through Jesus Christ our Lord. **Amen.**

FOURTH SUNDAY OF ADVENT

Opening Sentences

Mary will bear a son and he shall be named Jesus, for he will save his people from their sins. He will be great, and of his kingdom there will be no end.

Prayer of Adoration

God, the rock of our salvation, you are utterly dependable.
We rejoice in your covenant love,
your faithfulness to all generations.
You are the God of Sarah and of Abraham, of Mary and of Joseph,
the God and Father of our Lord Jesus Christ.
In him you have set before us
the pattern for human life according to your will.
His coming dispels the darkness of our night
and offers us a new and living hope,
for he is Immanuel, God-with-us, now and for ever. **Amen.**

Prayer of Confession

Gracious God,
we recall at this time
those who prepared the way for the coming of your Son into the world.

Joseph awoke from sleep and did as the angel of the Lord commanded him.
We confess that we find it hard to be obedient to your voice.
Silence
In your tender mercy,
forgive us.

Mary said, 'Here am I, the Lord's servant.
Let it be with me according to your word.'
We confess that we prefer to make our own decisions and plans for the future.
Silence
In your tender mercy,
forgive us.

John the Baptist bore witness to one greater than himself.
We confess that our lives only dimly reflect the light of Christ.
Silence
In your tender mercy,
forgive us.

Here is good news for all who repent.
Jesus says: 'Your sins are forgiven.'
Thanks be to God. **Amen.**

Prayer of Thanksgiving

God our Father, creator of all, we thank you for your love.
You implanted within us a desire to understand the world in which
we live
and to know the one who created us.
You have not left us to grope in darkness for knowledge of your truth,
but have revealed your nature to us in your Son, Jesus Christ our Lord.

Lord Jesus Christ, Saviour and Brother, we thank you for your love.
Child of Mary, Bread of Life, Light of the World and Prince of Peace,
you lived our life and died our death.
Raised in glory, you live for ever and your kingdom will never end.
Through the Spirit, sent in your name,
you give us strength to serve you.

Holy Spirit, Spirit of Christ, we thank you for your love.
You are ever at work in the Church and in us,
inspiring, leading, enabling.
You breathe into us the life of Christ;
you help us in our weakness.

Father, Son and Holy Spirit, God of our salvation,
to you be glory, majesty, power and authority,
now and for ever. **Amen.**

Prayer of Dedication

Generous God, from whom all blessings flow,
we can give you only what you have first given to us.
Thankful for all your goodness and ready to do your will,
we offer ourselves again to you.
We are your servants; may your will be fulfilled in us;
through Jesus Christ our Lord. **Amen.**

CHRISTMAS DAY

Opening Sentences

The Word became flesh and lived among us. And we have seen his glory.

Prayer of Approach and Adoration

Gracious God,
we come into your presence with joy and wonder
to declare your glory
and celebrate your marvellous works.
For you are high over all the earth
and greatly to be praised,
yet you have come to us in Jesus,
your eternal Word,
and saved us according to your mercy.
He is the reflection of your splendour,
the imprint of your being,
the heir of all things,
through whom you created the worlds.
Born among us, helpless, dependent,
emptied of his majesty,
being's source began to be;
and we have seen his glory,
full of grace and truth.

Glory to God in the highest;
through Jesus Christ our Lord. **Amen.**

Prayer of Confession

God, whose glory has been revealed to the world
in Jesus Christ your Son,
forgive us if we have obscured the meaning of Christmas
by wrong priorities, foolish anxieties,
feverish activity and festive indulgence.
Draw us again to the light of Christ,
which shines in our darkness,
and teach us to live in accordance with your will;

through him, in whom your grace has appeared,
bringing salvation for all,
our Saviour Jesus Christ. **Amen.**

Prayer of Thanksgiving

Blessèd are you, eternal God,
creator of the universe,
source of life and light.
You made this world of beauty and splendour
and us in your image and likeness.
Despite our selfishness and sin,
you have never ceased to love us
but have given your Son, Jesus Christ,
to save us from ourselves
and to draw us close to you.
He, the eternal Word,
through whom you made all things,
became flesh and lived among us
and in him is life and light for all the world.
We thank you for the good news of his coming,
his life and death and resurrection,
his reign at your right hand
and the gift of the Holy Spirit,
whom you have sent in his name.
With joyful hearts we give you thanks and praise
through Jesus Christ our Lord. **Amen.**

Prayer of Dedication

Eternal God,
your Son laid aside the glory of heaven
and was born in a humble stable.
Accept the gifts which we offer now
as tokens of our thankfulness,
and accept our lives,
dedicated to your service.
We ask it for the sake of Jesus. **Amen.**

FIRST SUNDAY OF CHRISTMAS

Opening Sentence

When the fullness of time had come, God sent his Son, born of a woman, born under the law.

Prayer of Adoration

Great and wonderful God,
creator and ruler of all,
your ways are just and true
and you alone are holy.
Your Son Jesus Christ is the pioneer of our salvation,
who became like us in every respect
that we might share the life divine.
Loving, saving, gracious God,
we rejoice in you with our whole being
and bless your holy name;
through Jesus Christ our Lord. **Amen.**

Prayer of Confession

Merciful God,
you reach out to us with compassion
and grace which we do not deserve.
We are arrogant and self-obsessed,
complacent and self-satisfied.
We have turned away from you
and followed our own paths.
Yet in your love and pity
you have redeemed us
through your Son Jesus Christ.
He brings light to overcome our darkness,
and grace to cover all our sin.
In his name we turn to you in confidence and faith
and ask you to forgive us for his sake. **Amen.**

Prayer of Thanksgiving

God of all-redeeming grace,
we give you thanks for your mighty deeds
and all that you have done for us
in your abundant love.
You sent no messenger or angel to our race
but in Christ you became present to save us.
He was born among us,
sharing our flesh and blood,
and was nurtured by Mary and Joseph.
He grew and became strong,
increasing in wisdom and in years.
Baptized in the Jordan, at one with us,
he proclaimed your kingdom
in powerful acts of grace and love.
Lifted up on the Cross,
he shared our human death,
and conquered death for ever.
Raised again triumphant,
he reigns with you in glory
and prays for us eternally.
His Spirit guides and teaches us
and unites us in Christ's body, the Church.
For all your mighty deeds,
we give you thanks and praise;
through Jesus Christ our Lord. **Amen.**

Prayer of Dedication

Lord our God,
we bring our gifts and our lives
and with gratitude in our hearts
we offer them to you;
in the name of him who was born for us
and died for us,
our Saviour Jesus Christ. **Amen.**

SECOND SUNDAY OF CHRISTMAS

Opening Sentences

No one has ever seen God. It is God the Son, who is close to the Father's heart, who has made him known.

Prayer of Approach and Adoration

God, immortal, invisible,
hidden from our eyes,
yet revealed to us in Jesus,
we worship and adore you.
We come with joyful hearts
to celebrate his birth;
we come to confess our sins;
we come to listen to your voice;
we come to give you thanks
and dedicate our lives to you;
we come to pray for others and ourselves.
May this act of worship be to your glory;
through Jesus Christ our Lord. **Amen.**

Prayer of Confession

We are not worthy, holy God,
to come into your presence,
for we have been foolish and disobedient.
We have gone our own way,
sought our own comfort,
and lived as though we had no need of you.
And yet we know that we depend on your grace,
that without you our lives have no meaning.
For the sake of your Son, Jesus Christ,
who became a little child,
forgive our many sins
and help us to walk in humility before you.
We ask it in his name. **Amen.**

Prayer of Thanksgiving

Eternal God,
you made us in your wisdom
and your Son Jesus Christ died for us in love.
We rejoice in you
and bless your holy name.

Before the foundation of the world,
you chose us in Christ
to be holy and blameless before you
and, though we marred your image in us,
you reconciled us to yourself in Christ.
We rejoice in you
and bless your holy name.

Through him we have been adopted as your children
and of his fullness we have all received,
grace upon grace.
He, who is close to your heart, has made you known.
We rejoice in you
and bless your holy name.

Born in Bethlehem, baptized in the Jordan,
crucified at Calvary, glorious in heaven,
he is Immanuel, God-with-us,
ever-present through the Spirit to renew our life.
We rejoice in you
and bless your holy name;

through Jesus Christ our Lord. **Amen.**

Prayer of Dedication

We delight in you, our God;
we thank you for your abundant goodness,
and for the gift of Jesus Christ, your Son.
As we bring our gifts,
we offer ourselves to live and work
to your glory and praise;
in the name of Christ our Lord. **Amen.**

THE EPIPHANY

These prayers may be used on the preceding Sunday if 6 January is a weekday.

Opening Sentence

From the rising of the sun to its setting, my name is great among the nations, says the Lord.

Prayer of Adoration

Eternal God, yours is the glory,
the majesty, the power and the authority;
and everything in heaven and on earth is yours.
We worship and adore you; we praise your holy name.

In every age you have given to the human race
glimpses of your glory,
the glory that was fully shown in Jesus Christ your Son.
For he is your eternal Word, through whom all things were made;
and the Word was made flesh and lived among us,
and we have seen his glory, full of grace and truth.

Eternal God, revealed to us in Jesus,
we worship and adore you; we praise your holy name;
through Jesus Christ our Lord. **Amen.**

Prayer of Confession

Living God,
we are sorry for all that is wrong in our lives.
Forgive our disobedience, our selfishness, our pride,
and, by your Spirit's guiding light,
lead us again to Jesus,
that we may learn from him and follow in his way.
We ask it for his sake. **Amen.**

Prayer of Thanksgiving

Eternal God,
your mercy and grace reach out to all the world.
You deliver the needy when they call,
the poor and those who have no helper.
You loved the world so much that you sent your only Son
that through him the world might be saved.
Through his birth, his life, his death and his resurrection
he displayed your love for everyone.
We celebrate your wonderful deeds.
We give you thanks and praise.

We thank you that, when Jesus was born,
not only shepherds from the fields nearby
but also wise men from the east came to worship him;
and that Simeon recognized in him not only the glory of Israel
but also the Light to lighten the Gentiles.
We thank you for calling together in the one body of Christ
people of all races and nations
to share in the boundless riches of Christ.
We celebrate your wonderful deeds.
We give you thanks and praise.

We thank you for the Church's calling
to proclaim the good news throughout the world,
to serve and love in the name of Christ,
and to care for all without reserve.
We thank you for the Holy Spirit, our enabler and guide,
by whose strength alone the Church is sustained.
We celebrate your wonderful deeds.
We give you thanks and praise;
through Jesus Christ our Lord. **Amen.**

Prayer of Dedication

Generous God,
as we rejoice in your great kindness to us,
we humbly offer to you our gifts, our hearts, ourselves,
and pray that, empowered by your Spirit,
we may live to your glory and praise;
through Jesus Christ our Lord. **Amen.**

SUNDAY BETWEEN 7 AND 13 JANUARY

Sunday after Epiphany

First Sunday in Ordinary Time

Opening Sentences

God says: Do not be afraid; I have redeemed you. I have called you by name; you are mine.

Prayer of Approach and Adoration

'Ascribe to the Lord glory and strength;
ascribe to the Lord the glory of his name.'

We come into your presence,
glorious Lord of heaven and earth,
to worship and adore you.
Empower us by your Holy Spirit
that we may worship you as you deserve,
with joy and with reverence,
in spirit and in truth;
for the sake of Jesus Christ our Lord. **Amen.**

Prayer of Confession

God most holy,
we sinners turn to you in penitence,
confessing our many sins.
Your Son is a Light to the nations,
but we have walked in darkness.
He came to open eyes that are blind,
but we have failed to see him
in the neighbours from whom we turn aside.
We marvel at the knowledge that, despite our sinful nature,
we are precious in your sight.
Forgive us, we pray,
and help us to live as those who have died to sin
and risen with Christ to newness of life;
for we ask it in his name. **Amen.**

Prayer of Thanksgiving

God, who created the heavens and the earth,
you are the source of our life.
When we forsake you, you seek us out,
When we return to you, you are gentle and merciful.
Your Son came to be our Saviour,
taking our nature upon him.
He was baptized by John in the Jordan,
identifying himself with sinners,
not turning aside from humankind
but meeting us in our need.
He shared our death on the Cross
and was raised by your mighty power.
Through baptism and the Holy Spirit
we are born again in him,
united within his body,
and called to share in his mission.
Baptized into his death,
we have victory over death through him.
United with him in a resurrection like his,
we rejoice in the glorious hope
that we shall live with him for ever.
To him, with you and your life-giving Spirit,
be all honour and glory,
now and for ever. **Amen.**

Prayer of Dedication

Eternal God,
you have given us new life
through baptism and the Holy Spirit.
We dedicate ourselves again to you,
and pray that we may be your faithful servants
to the end of our lives;
through Jesus Christ our Lord. **Amen.**

SUNDAY BETWEEN 14 AND 20 JANUARY

Second Sunday in Ordinary Time

Opening Sentence

Grace to you and peace from God our Father and the Lord Jesus Christ.

Prayer of Adoration

Faithful God,
your steadfast love knows no limit;
your righteousness is like mighty mountains;
your judgements are like the great deep.
Before we were born, you knew us;
throughout our lives you have loved us;
you are acquainted with all our ways.
You are the fountain of life
and in your light we see light.
All praise and honour belong to you,
now and for ever;
through Jesus Christ our Lord. **Amen.**

Prayer of Confession

God of truth and grace,
we cannot escape from your presence.
We cannot hide our sin from you,
for you have searched us and known us;
you see us more clearly than we see ourselves.
We humbly confess the wrong we have done
and the good we have failed to do.
As we come to you in penitence,
assure us of your pardoning love
and write your law within our hearts
that we may delight to do your will;
through Jesus Christ our Lord. **Amen.**

Prayer of Thanksgiving

None can compare with you, our God;
your wondrous deeds are more than can be counted.
In the beginning, you created the universe
and your mighty hand holds it in being.
When we wandered from your ways
you sent your Son, our Saviour Christ,
to bring us back to you.
He is the Lamb of God
who takes away the sin of the world.
He lived and died and was raised again
that we might have life in all its fullness
and your salvation might reach to the ends of the earth.
Through the Holy Spirit,
whom you sent in his name,
you have called the Church into being,
showering upon us a variety of gifts
and moulding us into one body,
equipping us to witness and serve
and guiding us on our journey.
None can compare with you, our God;
your wondrous deeds are more than can be counted.
All praise and thanks be given to you,
with the Son and the Spirit,
in time and in all eternity. **Amen.**

Prayer of Dedication

God, rich in mercy,
we are not our own, but yours,
for we have been bought with a price.
We bring our gifts and dedicate our lives to you,
in the name of him who died for us,
yet is alive and reigns with you and the Holy Spirit,
Jesus Christ our Lord. **Amen.**

SUNDAY BETWEEN 21 AND 27 JANUARY

Third Sunday in Ordinary Time

Opening Sentence

Let the words of our mouths and the meditation of our hearts be acceptable in your sight, O Lord, our rock and our redeemer.

Prayer of Approach and Adoration

The heavens proclaim your glory, Lord;
creation resounds to your praise.
Your law is perfect, reviving the soul;
your decrees are sure, making wise the simple.
You are our light and salvation,
the strength of our lives.
We come into your house as guests invited by you
and we offer you our worship.
Blessing and honour and glory and power
be yours for ever and ever. **Amen.**

Prayer of Confession

God of all mercy,
we confess to you that we are sinners
and members of a sinful race.
In silence we acknowledge before you the sins of which we are aware.

Silence

We also confess to you our secret faults, known to you alone.

Silence

Assure us of your love and forgiveness
that we may know your joy and peace
and worship you now in spirit and in truth;
through Jesus Christ our Lord. **Amen.**

Prayer of Thanksgiving

We thank you, gracious God,
for your love for all creation.
In compassion and goodness,
you reach out to all people
and forgive the sins of those who are penitent.
You show no partiality; you have no favourites.

We thank you for Jesus,
who came to bring good news to the poor
and recovery of sight to the blind.
We thank you for the first disciples,
who responded to his call and left their nets to follow him,
and for the bright succession of your faithful servants.

We thank you that Jesus, crucified, risen and ascended,
is the head of his body, the Church,
into which we are all baptized in the one Spirit,
whether Jew or Gentile, slave or free,
and called to be united in the same mind and the same purpose,
to share in your mission throughout the world.

For all that you have done for us
we thank you and we praise you,
in the name of our Saviour, Jesus Christ your Son. **Amen.**

Prayer of Dedication

God of love,
accept the gifts we bring to you,
accept the prayers we make to you,
accept the lives we give to you,
and use them all to your glory;
through Jesus Christ our Lord. **Amen.**

SUNDAY BETWEEN 28 JANUARY AND 3 FEBRUARY

Fourth Sunday in Ordinary Time

Opening Sentences

The fear of the Lord is the beginning of wisdom; all those who practise it have a good understanding. His praise endures for ever.

Prayer of Approach and Adoration

Eternal God, the source of all life,
great and wonderful are your works,
full of honour and majesty.
We come before you humbly,
for holy and awesome is your name
and we are weak and sinful.
Yet we also come with confidence,
for you are gracious and merciful,
and you have shown us in Jesus
a love which never ends.
You are our rock, our refuge,
our fortress strong to save.
Glory and praise be yours for ever;
through Jesus Christ our Lord. **Amen.**

Prayer of Confession

God of grace and mercy,
you have created us
and called us to live blamelessly
and do what is right,
to act justly, love kindness,
and walk humbly with you, our God.
We confess that our lives have fallen short of our calling.
We have done what is wrong
and failed to do what is right.
We have acted unjustly and unkindly;
we have been arrogant and proud.
In your abundant mercy,
forgive what we have been and done,

and help us to live in the power of your Spirit,
to the glory of your name;
through Jesus Christ our Lord. **Amen.**

Prayer of Thanksgiving

God, our Father and our Mother,
you brought the universe to birth
and you knew us before we were born.
All wisdom and knowledge,
all strength and power,
derive from you alone.

In Jesus Christ, your Son,
you have shown us the true nature of wisdom and strength.
He was born in a humble stable,
he died a cruel death;
yet in him we see the weakness which is stronger than human strength,
and the foolishness that is wiser than all our human wisdom.
We thank you that Christ is risen and alive
and that in the Church which is his body
you have chosen what is weak and foolish, low and despised,
to fulfil your glorious purposes.
We thank you for the Holy Spirit,
ever at work in the world,
who helps us in our prayers
and strengthens us to live in love for one another and for you.
For all your acts of grace and love,
we give you thanks and praise;
through Jesus Christ our Lord. **Amen.**

Prayer of Dedication

O God, what offering can we give to you,
the Lord of heaven and earth?
We bring our gifts as tokens of our thanks
and we offer ourselves for your service.
Make us pure in heart, merciful and meek,
eager for righteousness, makers of peace,
that we may be truly blessed
and bring blessing to others;
for the sake of Christ our Saviour. **Amen.**

SUNDAY BETWEEN 4 AND 10 FEBRUARY

Fifth Sunday in Ordinary Time

Opening Sentence

Holy, holy, holy is the Lord of hosts; the whole earth is full of his glory.

Prayer of Approach and Adoration

Everlasting God,
creator of the ends of the earth,
you do not faint or grow tired;
you give power to the weary
and strengthen the powerless.
You heal the broken-hearted
and bind up their wounds.
Your understanding is unsearchable;
your steadfast love endures for ever.
You are worthy of nobler worship than we can offer,
yet you do not despise the lowly.
How good it is to sing your praise;
for you are great and gracious.
To you we ascribe all honour and glory;
through Jesus Christ our Lord. **Amen.**

Prayer of Confession

Holy God,
we confess with shame
our share in the sin of humankind
that crucified the Lord of glory.
In him you have given us life and joy
and you call us in Christ
to be lights for the world,
but we hide your light from others.
Forgive all that is wrong in our lives
and remake us in your image and likeness;
for the sake of him

who died and rose again for us,
our Saviour, Jesus Christ. **Amen.**

Prayer of Thanksgiving

Eternal Wisdom, God most high,
we bless you for your wonderful works.
You made the world in beauty and splendour;
creation resounds to your glory.
You created us, male and female, in your own image
and did not abandon us when we sinned against you.
We remember with thankfulness
the life on earth of your Son, Jesus Christ,
who proclaimed your kingdom
and healed the sick.
He died for our sins and was buried
and you raised him again on the third day.
Through him you have sent your life-giving Spirit
to teach us and lead us into truth
and enable us to serve in the Church and the world.
We thank you for all the faithful in every age,
who have responded to Christ's call,
reflected his light
and walked in his way.
Especially we bless you for those who have inspired us
on our journey of faith;
and we pray that you will bring us, with them,
to the joy of your eternal kingdom;
through Jesus Christ our Lord. **Amen.**

Prayer of Dedication

The whole earth is full of your glory, Lord,
and all that is good comes from you.
Receive these gifts, which we offer with love,
and grant that our lives may bring honour to you;
for the sake of Jesus our Lord. **Amen.**

SUNDAY BETWEEN 11 AND 17 FEBRUARY

Sixth Sunday in Ordinary Time

Opening Sentence

Sing praises to the Lord and give thanks to his holy name.

Prayer of Adoration

Glorious beyond our sense of majesty,
holy beyond our sense of purity,
merciful beyond our sense of compassion,
you are God, and we praise you.
You reign supreme beyond time and space,
in beauty and splendour and light.
We adore you, O God;
we praise your great name;
we offer you worship;
through Jesus Christ our Lord. **Amen.**

Prayer of Confession

'Great is the wisdom of the Lord; he is mighty in power and sees everything.'

Great and wise God,
nothing can be hidden from your sight.
You test the mind and search the heart
and you know our human frailty.
We have turned away from you
and put our trust in gods of our own making.
Our delight has not been in your law;
we have been jealous and quarrelsome,
selfish and greedy,
foolish and proud.
We seek your forgiveness.
Hear us, O God, and be gracious to us.
Restore to us the joy of your salvation,
that we may trust in you

and seek to do your will;
through Jesus Christ our Lord. **Amen.**

Prayer of Thanksgiving

All-gracious God,
it is our duty and delight
to give you thanks and praise.
Blessed are those who trust in you.
They are like trees planted by the water,
sending out their roots into the stream
of your eternal love.
We thank you for the revelation of that love
in Jesus Christ our Lord.
He lived among us and endured the Cross
and you have raised him from the dead,
to be the first-fruits of those who sleep.
We thank you for the glorious hope
that you have set before us
and the gifts of the Spirit,
showered upon the Church.
To you, gracious God,
in the power of the Spirit,
we ascribe all worship and glory and honour;
in the name of Jesus Christ, your Son, our Lord. **Amen.**

Prayer of Dedication

Generous God,
we offer to you the songs of our lips,
the love of our hearts,
the work of our hands,
and the service of our lives.
Empower us by your Holy Spirit
that we may walk in your ways
and hold fast to you;
through Jesus Christ our Lord. **Amen.**

SUNDAY BETWEEN 18 AND 24 FEBRUARY

Seventh Sunday in Ordinary Time

Opening Sentence

Lord, teach us the way of your statutes; lead us in the path of your commandments.

Prayer of Approach and Adoration

Heaven and earth are full of your glory,
almighty, eternal, most holy God.
You deserve the adoration of every creature;
you are worthy of worship and honour and love.
Accept the praise we offer;
and grant that, as we hear your word
and rejoice in the presence of your Holy Spirit,
we may glimpse your glory
in the face of your Son Jesus Christ,
in whom we make our prayer. **Amen.**

Prayer of Confession

Lord our God,
be gracious to us and heal us,
for we have sinned against you.

You have called us to be holy
as you yourself are holy.
We confess the impurity and unrighteousness of our lives.
We have exalted ourselves
when we should have been humble;
given in to temptation
when we should have resisted;
and pleased ourselves
when we should have pleased you.
Lord, have mercy upon us.

You have called us to love our neighbours
as we love ourselves.

We confess that we have been angry
when we should have shown compassion,
we have been selfish
when we should have been generous,
we have been indifferent
when we should have helped.
Lord, have mercy upon us.

Lord our God,
be gracious to us and heal us;
through Jesus Christ our Lord. **Amen.**

Prayer of Thanksgiving

God of love,
you send sun and rain on the just and the unjust;
you are kind to the ungrateful and the wicked.
You show no partiality.
We rejoice in your bountiful goodness
and thank you for your mercy.

In Jesus Christ your love for all was made visible in the world.
His life and death and resurrection proclaim your truth and grace.
Exalted in glory in heaven,
he ever prays for us;
and you have given the Holy Spirit
to build us into a living temple,
whose foundation is Christ himself,
that we may offer spiritual sacrifices to you.

For all these signs of your goodness and grace,
accept our praise and thanks;
through Christ our Lord. **Amen.**

Prayer of Dedication

Loving God, maker of all,
we dedicate ourselves again to you.
Give us understanding,
that we may keep your law of love
and observe it with all our heart;
and keep us faithful in your service, now and always;
for the sake of Jesus Christ, your Son. **Amen.**

SUNDAY BETWEEN 25 AND 29 FEBRUARY

Eighth Sunday in Ordinary Time

Opening Sentences

Sing for joy, O heavens, and exult, O earth. For the Lord has comforted his people.

Prayer of Approach

As we come into your presence,
God of our salvation,
help us to calm and quieten our spirits.
Open our eyes, that we may catch sight of your glory.
Open our ears, that we may hear your word.
Open our hearts, that we may respond in love;
through Jesus Christ our Lord. **Amen.**

Prayer of Confession

Compassionate God,
your Son Jesus Christ came to call
not the righteous, but sinners.
We confess that we are sinners
and we seek your forgiveness
for the times when we have called Jesus 'Lord'
but not done what he commands;
for the times when we have seen the speck in another's eye
but been blind to the log in our own;
for the times when we have been slow to forgive
but quick to take offence.
In steadfast love and mercy,
listen to our prayer.
Pardon our transgressions
and strengthen us by your Spirit.
We ask it for Christ's sake. **Amen.**

Prayer of Thanksgiving

'Bless the Lord, O my soul; and all that is within me, bless his holy name.'

It is good to give thanks to you, O God,
to praise your name, O Most High.
You created the heavens and the earth
and saw that they were good.
You made us for yourself
and when, in our folly and disobedience,
we turned away from you,
you did not abandon us
but sought us in your love.

We give you thanks for the victory
which you give us in the Lord Jesus Christ;
for in his life and death and resurrection
he has conquered sin and death for us,
and through our baptism we share in his risen life.

We thank you for our place within the Church,
for nourishment in word and sacrament,
and for our calling to be servants of Christ
and stewards of your mysteries,
with your Spirit at work within us,
moving us to worship and witness.
All praise and thanks be given to you,
through Jesus Christ your Son,
in the unity of the Holy Spirit
now and for ever. **Amen.**

Prayer of Dedication

Giving thanks for all your goodness,
we bring our gifts to you, O God,
and offer ourselves in your service.
Help us to be faithful and fruitful in this life
and, by your mercy,
bring us with your saints
to your eternal kingdom;
through Jesus Christ our Lord. **Amen.**

SUNDAY BEFORE LENT

Opening Sentence

God, who said 'Let light shine out of darkness', has shone in our hearts to give the light of the knowledge of his glory in the face of Jesus Christ.

Prayer of Approach and Adoration

God of glory and God of grace,
source of life and maker of light,
radiant in splendour, resplendent in beauty,
we praise and adore you.
Let your light shine upon us now,
revealing your glory and mercy and love,
that we may be lifted out of ourselves
into the light and joy of your presence
and worship you with our whole being;
through Jesus Christ our Lord. **Amen.**

Prayer of Confession

Holy God,
as we contemplate the wonder and perfection of your being,
we call to mind our own sin and weakness.
We confess that our heavenly vision is dimmed by self-regard;
our obedience to your will is overruled by self-indulgence;
our compassion is obstructed by self-centredness.

Forgive us that, in our folly and our blindness,
we lead impoverished lives
when the immeasurable riches of your grace in Christ
are offered freely to all who trust in him.
Holy God, forgive our sins;
lighten our darkness;
strengthen us by your Spirit;
and give us peace;
for the sake of Jesus Christ our Light. **Amen.**

Prayer of Thanksgiving

God, who in the beginning created light
and separated it from darkness,
you are the source of all knowledge and truth.
You made a covenant with the people of Israel,
and, when they wandered from your ways,
you sent the prophets,
with a message like a lamp shining in a dark place,
to recall your people to yourself.
God of light,
we give you thanks and praise.

In the fullness of time, you sent Jesus Christ,
the Sun of Righteousness,
to be the Light of the World.
On the holy mountain,
his disciples glimpsed his glory,
when his face shone with heavenly brightness
and he was revealed as your belovèd Son.
God of light,
we give you thanks and praise.

Obedient to your will,
he died on the Cross.
Raised in resurrection glory,
he lives for ever in splendour and majesty.
His Spirit enlightens us,
leading us into the truth
and illuminating the path before us.
God of light,
we give you thanks and praise;

through Jesus Christ our Lord. **Amen.**

Prayer of Dedication

Help us to love you, Lord,
and give our lives to you.
Help us to serve you, Lord,
and give ourselves to others.
Help us to praise you, Lord,
and give you all the glory;
through Jesus Christ our Lord. **Amen.**

ASH WEDNESDAY

Opening Sentences

Rend your hearts and not your garments. Return to the Lord your God, for he is gracious and merciful.

Prayer of Approach and Adoration

Eternal God,
most blessèd and most holy,
before the brightness of whose presence the angels veil their faces,
we are not worthy to lift our eyes to your glory.
And yet in your grace and love
you are pleased to accept our worship.
Lost in wonder, love and praise,
we come before you now.
All glory be to you, in time and in eternity;
in Jesus Christ our Saviour. **Amen.**

Prayer of Confession

Merciful God,
you are slow to anger and abounding in steadfast love.
Have mercy on us, sinners that we are,
and members of a fallen race.
You created us to love and serve you,
but we have been selfish and disobedient.
You have spoken to us again and again,
but we have ignored your message.
You sent your Son, the Saviour of the world,
but we rejected and crucified him.
You gave your Holy Spirit to be our guide,
but we have not listened to his promptings.
You have made us members of a royal priesthood,
but our worship has been cold and half-hearted.
You have sought to nurture us in knowledge and holiness,
but we have neglected the means of grace.
You have given us other people to care for and love,
but we have turned away from them.

Silence

Our sin is great and grievous.
Yet your mercy, O God, is greater.
We hear Christ's word of grace: Your sins are forgiven.
Thanks be to God. **Amen.**

Prayer of Thanksgiving

God our maker and redeemer,
we thank you for creating the universe
and for giving your Son to be our Saviour.
We thank you for your undeserved love for the world,
displayed in Christ's life and death and resurrection and ascension,
and in the gift of the Holy Spirit, our advocate and guide.
Especially at this time we thank you
for the challenge which Christ continues to present
to our conceitedness and complacency,
our dishonesty and selfishness.
We thank you that he always spoke the truth,
and that he was obedient to your will,
though obedience led him to the Cross.
We thank you that, through your holy Church,
you have given us this solemn season of Lent
as a time when we can examine our lives
and measure them against the standard of Christ.
Merciful, holy, redeeming God,
we praise you and we thank you;
in the name of our Saviour Jesus Christ. **Amen.**

Prayer of Dedication

Yours we are, eternal God,
created and saved by your love.
We dedicate ourselves again to you,
praying that you will show us, by the Spirit of truth,
the depth of our inbred sin;
that you will help us, by the Spirit of wisdom,
to be honest in our estimation of ourselves;
that you will enable us, by the Spirit of power,
to live more nearly as we pray;
and that you will bring us at last, by the Spirit of life,
to the peace and joy of your kingdom;
for the sake of Jesus Christ our Lord. **Amen.**

FIRST SUNDAY IN LENT

Opening Sentence

Christ suffered for sins, once for all, the righteous for the unrighteous,
to bring us to God.

Prayer of Adoration

God immortal, God invisible, far beyond our human thought,
we praise you for revealing yourself as Father, Son and Holy Spirit,
Three Persons, and yet one God.

God the Father, you made us for yourself
and our hearts are restless till they find their rest in you.
In love and grace you sent your Son to be our Saviour.
To you be all glory and praise.

God the Son, for our salvation
you came to this earth and lived a life of love.
You died on the Cross, rose from the dead,
and promised us the gift of the Holy Spirit.
To you be all glory and praise.

God the Spirit, you come into our lives,
transforming, renewing and strengthening,
guiding us into Christ's way.
You call us into the life of faith and gather us into the body of Christ.
To you be all glory and praise.

Triune God, we worship and adore you.
To you be all glory and praise, now and for ever. **Amen.**

Prayer of Confession

God of our salvation,
your Son fasted for forty days in the desert
and, when he faced temptation, he triumphed over it.
We confess that, unlike Jesus, we yield to temptation and sin.

We confess our preoccupation with material things,
with money and food and possessions.

We admit that our ears have been deaf to your call
and that we have not been obedient to your words.
We confess our reluctance to live by faith,
our longing to know all the answers.
We admit that our spirits have longed for security
and that we have not fully trusted in you.
We confess our obsession with greatness and strength,
with wealth and renown and success.
We admit that our eyes have been dazzled by power
and that we have not sought to serve you alone.

God of our salvation, forgive us all our sins.
Lead us in your truth and teach us;
through Jesus Christ our Lord. **Amen.**

Prayer of Thanksgiving

Generous God, whose grace reaches out to all,
we thank you for your mighty acts.
Your sovereign love extends to every creature
and you have accomplished the salvation of the world
in Jesus Christ, your Son.
Though he was with you before the universe was created
and through him all things were made,
he came and dwelt among us, sharing our human life.
Tested in the desert, he triumphed over temptation.
Dying on the Cross, he conquered sin and death.
Raised to life in glory, he prays for us for ever.
In our weakness, you do not leave us alone,
but have sent the Holy Spirit to help us in our prayers
and in our mission to share the good news with others.
For all your mighty acts, we give you thanks and praise;
through Jesus Christ our Lord. **Amen.**

Prayer of Dedication (based on a hymn by Charles Wesley)

In the strength of your grace, Lord God,
and with hearts that are glad and free,
we commit ourselves to your service alone,
for the rest of our lives;
in the name of Jesus Christ our Saviour. **Amen.**

SECOND SUNDAY IN LENT

Opening Sentence

Wait for the Lord; be strong, take heart.

Prayer of Approach and Adoration

Everlasting God,
the wonder of your being is beyond our understanding.
You were before all things were made;
and when this universe is no more,
you will still be,
God supreme, eternal, beyond time and space.
How can you spare a thought for us?

Yet you have taught us
that we are precious in your sight,
and that your mercy and love are limitless.
So hear us and be gracious
as we come to seek your face.
Look on us with kindness
and accept the praise we offer;
for we come in the name of your Son,
our Saviour Jesus Christ. **Amen.**

Prayer of Confession

God of compassion,
we confess that we are sinners.

In Jesus, you show us that it is better to give than to receive;
but we remain selfish and greedy.
In Jesus, you show us that love is stronger than hatred;
but we nurse grievances and resentment.
In Jesus, you show us a new way of living;
but we are content with the standards of the world.
In Jesus, you show us the way to true greatness;
but we are afraid to follow him.

Forgive us, God of compassion.
Assure us of your mercy and love.
Enable us by your Spirit's power

and grant that we may attain that fullness of life
which you offer in Christ our Lord.
We ask it for his sake. **Amen.**

Prayer of Thanksgiving

God, our light and our salvation,
creator of heaven and earth,
we thank you for making us in your own image
and for sending your Son, Jesus Christ,
not to condemn the world,
but that through him the world might be saved.
We thank you for the sufferings he endured
for the sake of humankind.
Tempted, rejected, betrayed and denied,
he died on the Cross that we may have life.
Raised by your power,
he reigns in glory,
yet intercedes for us eternally.
We thank you for the Holy Spirit,
the Lord, the giver of life;
for the Church, your new creation,
and for our place within it.
Grant that we may show our thankfulness,
not in words alone,
but by lives devoted to your service
and the service of others,
as we seek to follow in the way of your Son,
our Saviour Jesus Christ,
in whom we make our prayer. **Amen.**

Prayer of Dedication

Father God,
you loved the world so much
that you gave your only Son
so that those who believe in him should have everlasting life.
We cannot repay the debt we owe,
but we give you what we can.
Take us and use us to your glory;
for the sake of Jesus Christ our Lord. **Amen.**

THIRD SUNDAY IN LENT

Opening Sentence

God is spirit, and those who worship him must worship in spirit and in truth.

Prayer of Approach

O God, you are our God;
we seek you; our souls thirst for you,
as in a dry and weary land
where there is no water.
You alone can refresh and sustain us;
you alone are the fountain of life.
Grant that the living water which you give through your Son
may evermore rise up within us;
and grant that we may worship you now
in spirit and in truth;
through Jesus Christ our Lord. **Amen.**

Prayer of Confession

'My thoughts are not your thoughts, nor are your ways my ways, says the Lord.'

God, all-wise and all-loving,
we confess the irreverence and insincerity
which spoil the worship we offer:
we praise you with our lips,
while our thoughts are far from you.

And we confess the selfishness and pride
which spoil our human relationships:
we think chiefly of ourselves,
and are indifferent to the needs of others.
In your mercy,
pardon our offences
and cleanse our thoughts,
that the words of our mouths
and the meditation of our hearts

may be acceptable to you;
through Jesus Christ our Lord. **Amen.**

Prayer of Thanksgiving

In the beginning, eternal God,
you fashioned the earth and gave life to its people.
To you alone we owe our every breath.
We bless your holy name.

You have shown your love for us
in that, when we were far from you, you came to meet us
and, while we were still sinners, Christ died for us.
You raised him from death
to be our Lord and head,
and your love has been poured into our hearts
through the Holy Spirit whom you have given to us.
We bless your holy name.

You have gathered us together from every people and nation
to be a holy priesthood,
offering spiritual sacrifices to you,
and to love and serve our neighbours
in the name of Jesus Christ.
You give to us the privilege of sharing in your mission.
We bless your holy name.

For all your loving kindness,
we bless your holy name;
in Jesus Christ our Lord,
who lives and reigns with you and the Holy Spirit,
one God, for ever and ever. **Amen.**

Prayer of Dedication (based on a hymn by Charles Wesley)

God of almighty love,
we offer to you our gifts and our lives
through the ever-blessèd name of Jesus.
Grant that we may constantly
trust in your goodness
and live to your glory;
for the sake of Christ our Lord. **Amen.**

FOURTH SUNDAY IN LENT

Opening Sentence

In Christ, God was reconciling the world to himself, not counting our sins against us. Our God is a God of love

Prayer of Approach

God, our Shepherd,
whose goodness and mercy have followed us
all the days of our lives,
we approach you with joyful hearts.
Help us to worship you aright, with reverence and with wonder,
with confidence and with faith, with humility and with awe;
and may this sacrifice of praise be to your glory.
We ask it in the name of Jesus Christ our Lord. **Amen.**

Prayer of Confession

True and wise God, we cannot hide from your sight.
You see beyond outward appearance;
you know our inner motives; you read what is in our hearts.
We confess to you our preoccupation with ourselves,
our concern for our own comfort and security,
our carelessness as stewards of your gifts,
our thoughtlessness towards our neighbours,
our lack of compassion for those in need,
and our forgetfulness of you.
Forgive our sins, we humbly pray,
and help us to turn from darkness and live as children of light,
bearing fruit that is good and right and true;
through Jesus Christ our Lord. **Amen.**

Prayer of Thanksgiving

Let us offer to God our thanks, as we recall his deeds with joy.

Let us thank God for creation:
for his is the mind that conceived the galaxies,
the power that brought the universe into being,
the love that created order and beauty.

Silence
We give thanks to the Lord, for he is good;
his steadfast love endures for ever.

Let us thank God for our own being:
for he made us in his image and likeness
and gave us the power to appreciate beauty.
Silence
We give thanks to the Lord, for he is good;
his steadfast love endures for ever.

Let us thank God for the revelation in Jesus Christ, his Son:
for in Christ's birth and ministry and death,
his resurrection and ascension,
we see God's power and purpose, his mercy and grace.
Silence
We give thanks to the Lord, for he is good;
his steadfast love endures for ever.

Let us thank God for the gift of grace:
for by this we receive salvation through faith,
and become a new creation in Christ, by the power of the Holy Spirit.
Silence
We give thanks to the Lord, for he is good;
his steadfast love endures for ever.

Let us thank God for the faithful departed:
for his Spirit was at work in their lives,
and their witness continues to inspire us as we follow in their steps.
Silence
We give thanks to the Lord, for he is good;
his steadfast love endures for ever. Amen.

Prayer of Dedication

God, rich in mercy,
you gave your Son to be the Light of the world
and he has been lifted up that we may have life eternal.
Receive these symbols of our gratitude and our lives offered in your
service,
to the praise of your holy name;
through Jesus Christ our Lord. **Amen.**

MOTHERING SUNDAY

Opening Sentence

As a mother comforts her child, says God, so shall I comfort you.

Prayer of Approach and Adoration

Loving God,
like a mother you enfold us in your care.
You never forget us,
you never forsake us;
you are utterly dependable.
We come, with hymns and spiritual songs,
to offer our praise and prayers.
All glory be to you, loving God,
for ever and ever. **Amen.**

Prayer of Confession

Eternal God,
whose Son Jesus Christ
shared in the life of an earthly home,
we confess our sins to you.

We have not treated one another
with love and respect.
We have put ourselves first
and been inconsiderate.
Eternal God,
in your mercy, forgive us.

We have not treated one another
with kindness and compassion.
We have been quick to take offence
and slow to forgive.
Eternal God,
in your mercy, forgive us.

We have not given to you
the honour and praise you deserve.

We have been foolish and disobedient
and wandered far from you.
Eternal God,
in your mercy, forgive us.

Give us compassion, kindness, humility,
patience, meekness and gentleness,
that we may be clothed with that love
which binds everything together in perfect harmony;
through Jesus Christ our Lord. **Amen.**

Prayer of Thanksgiving

God, our Father and our Mother,
you brought us to birth
and your loving kindness surrounds us each day of our life.
We thank you for creating us, male and female,
in your image and likeness,
and for the blessings that come to us through our human relationships.
We thank you for Moses' mother, who protected her son,
and for Hannah, who dedicated Samuel to your service.
We thank you for Mary, mother of Jesus,
who treasured in her heart and pondered in her mind
the wonder of his being;
who brought him up and cared for him, and was with him when he died.
We thank you for the Church, our Mother,
in whose family we are nurtured and fed, taught and enriched.
And we thank you for Jesus, the Church's head,
who lived for us and died for us,
who was raised from the dead,
and who lives and reigns with you, in the unity of the Holy Spirit,
one God, now and for ever. **Amen.**

Prayer of Dedication

Faithful God,
to whose service the child Samuel was dedicated by his mother,
we offer to you our friendships and relationships,
and pray that, in them, we may fulfil your purposes
and bring strength and joy to others;
for the sake of Jesus Christ,
our brother and our friend. **Amen.**

FIFTH SUNDAY IN LENT

First Sunday of the Passion

Opening Sentences

Unless a grain of wheat falls into the earth and dies, it remains a single grain. If it dies, it bears much fruit.

Prayer of Approach and Adoration

We come to you, eternal God,
and offer you our praise.
Unsurpassed in majesty,
matchless in your holiness,
you have shown to us in Jesus
unconquerable love.
As we contemplate his Passion,
may your Spirit guide our prayers
that we may worship you
sincerely and in truth;
for Jesus' sake. **Amen.**

Prayer of Confession

God of compassion,
with whom is great power to redeem,
we acknowledge with penitence
what poor disciples of Jesus we are
and how slow to follow in his way.

Jesus forgave his enemies,
but we are vindictive and seek revenge.
Jesus never used force to fulfil his purposes,
but we want our own way, whatever the cost.
Jesus was silent before his accusers,
but we bluster and argue and squabble and fight.
Jesus prayed fervently for strength to resist evil
but we expect painless results from feeble efforts.

Forgive us, O God.
In your abundant mercy,
wash away our sins.

Create in us clean hearts
and put a new and right spirit within us.
We ask it in the name of your Son,
our Saviour Jesus Christ. **Amen.**

Prayer of Thanksgiving

God of power and might and grace,
you have done great things for us.
Blessèd be your name!

You created the universe out of nothing
and formed the human race for yourself,
that we might declare your praise.
Perverse and foolish though we strayed,
you sought us in your love
and gave your Son to be our Saviour.
We give thanks for his passion and death;
for his resurrection from the dead.
He has become the source of eternal salvation
for all who obey him,
our great High Priest,
who, once for all, has offered the perfect sacrifice for us.
He is the Resurrection and the Life,
and all who believe in him will never die.

All praise and thanks be given to you,
God of power and might and grace,
with your Son, our Saviour,
and the life-giving Spirit;
now and throughout eternity. **Amen.**

Prayer of Dedication

Gracious God,
you gave your Son
to live and die for the world.
We offer these gifts as signs of our love
and we pray that our lives
may be used to your glory;
through Jesus Christ our Lord. **Amen.**

SIXTH SUNDAY IN LENT

Second Sunday of the Passion OR Palm Sunday

Opening Sentences

Blessèd is he who comes in the name of the Lord. Hosanna in the highest!

Prayer of Approach and Adoration

Let us approach God with reverence and awe, and be silent in his presence.

Silence

Glory and praise to God, creator, redeemer, renewer,
Ancient of Days, fountain of life, giver of light and hope of the world.

Glory and praise to God, coming humbly in Jesus,
the King on a donkey, riding toward the Cross.

Glory and praise to God, coming today through the Spirit,
the Spirit of truth and gentleness, the Spirit of life and power.

Glory and praise to God, Father, Son and Holy Spirit,
eternally Three-in-One; one God for ever and ever. **Amen.**

Prayer of Confession

God of tender compassion,
be merciful and gracious to us.
Forgive the sins of your people
as we come to you now in penitence.
We name the name of Jesus
while our actions betray him.
We claim to be his disciples
while we disregard his teachings.
With our lips we sing 'Hosanna'
while our lives shout 'Crucify him'.
We talk of grace and mercy
while we fail to forgive others.

God of tender compassion,
be merciful and gracious to us.
Forgive the sins of your people;
through Jesus Christ our Lord. **Amen.**

Prayer of Thanksgiving

You are our God, and we will give you thanks.
You are our God, and we will extol you.
Your doings are marvellous in our eyes,
O God of our salvation!
We give you thanks for Christ your Son,
the eternal Word, in whom all things were created.
He emptied himself of all but love
and took the form of a slave.
He entered Jerusalem humbly, riding on a donkey,
and became obedient to death –
even death on a cross.
Therefore you have highly exalted him
and given him the name above every name,
so that at the name of Jesus every knee should bend,
and every tongue confess that Jesus Christ is Lord,
to your glory, God our Father.
We give you thanks for the Holy Spirit,
at work in the Church and the world,
for our calling to be Christ's disciples
and to share in his mission of love and service.
We worship you; we give you thanks;
we praise you for your glory;
through Jesus Christ our Lord. **Amen.**

Prayer of Dedication

Gracious God,
your Son our Saviour entered Jerusalem
and gave his life for the world.
With grateful hearts we dedicate ourselves to you.
Help us to take up our cross and follow Jesus,
that, sharing in his sufferings,
we may know the power of his resurrection.
We ask it for his sake. **Amen.**

GOOD FRIDAY

Opening Sentence

Since we have confidence to enter the sanctuary by the blood of Jesus, let us approach with a true heart, in full assurance of faith.

Prayer of Approach and Adoration

Ever-present God,
we come before you
with awe and wonder
as we recall your power and wisdom,
your holiness and majesty.
We marvel at your grace and love,
revealed in Christ our Saviour,
and bless you for his eternal sacrifice.
We worship and adore you in his name. **Amen.**

Prayer of Confession

Loving God,
we remember today
all that you have done for us in Jesus Christ.
We recall with wonder his death on the Cross
and confess with shame
our share in the sin of the world
for which Christ died.
We ask your forgiveness now,
that the judgement we deserve
may be tempered by the perfect self-giving of Calvary,
by your ceaseless, unexhausted love,
unmerited and free;
through the grace of Christ our Saviour. **Amen.**

Prayer of Thanksgiving

Almighty and everlasting God,
we give you thanks for the creation of the universe
and for the gift of life.
We thank you for the ways
in which you have revealed yourself to the world,
supremely in your Son, our Saviour Jesus Christ.
He came among us, full of grace and truth,
but he was despised and rejected,
and held of no account.
Oppressed and afflicted,
led like a lamb to the slaughter,
he was lifted up on the Cross
to draw the whole creation to himself.
You raised him from the dead
and he reigns with you in glory.
Our great high priest, who has been tested, as we are,
and who is able to sympathize with our weakness,
he ever lives to pray for us.
For all your mighty acts of grace and love
we give you thanks and praise;
through Jesus Christ our Lord. **Amen.**

Prayer of Dedication (based on John Wesley's translation of a hymn by Paul Gerhardt)

Christ our Saviour,
we cannot repay the mighty debt we owe you.
We can never give you too much
or do too much for you.
May your love and your grief
be eternally engraved on our hearts,
and may our offering of all we have and are
be to your glory. **Amen.**

EASTER DAY

Opening Sentences

Alleluia! Christ is risen!
He is risen indeed! Alleluia!

Prayer of Approach and Adoration

Eternal God,
with gladness in our hearts
and songs on our lips
we come into your house this Easter Day
to worship you
and celebrate your mightiest act –
the raising of Jesus Christ from the dead.

We praise you that death could not hold him,
for you raised him up triumphant,
to greet his incredulous disciples,
convincing them that he was the same Jesus
who was dead but is alive for evermore,
changing their sorrow into joy
and giving them new life and hope.

We too are his disciples.
May the risen Christ be in our midst,
in power and love,
as we offer you our worship.
We ask it in his name. **Amen.**

Prayer of Confession

For our little faith,
gracious God,
forgive us.

For our little hope,
gracious God,
forgive us.

For our little love,
gracious God,
forgive us.

Increase in us your gifts of faith and hope and love,
and fill us with the joy and peace
that come from the knowledge that Christ is risen.
We ask it for his sake. **Amen.**

Prayer of Thanksgiving

God, our creator and redeemer,
we thank you for springtime –
earth released from the icy grip of winter,
green blades of wheat rising through the dark earth,
flowers in hedgerow and garden,
trees in bud, blossom ready to break,
lambs in the field, fledglings in the nest –
everywhere the promise of new life.

We thank you for the gift of your Son,
our Saviour Jesus Christ,
who became truly human,
lived a life of love and service,
and died for all upon the Cross.
We thank you that it was in a garden in springtime
that you raised him again,
the Lord of life, triumphant over death.
We thank you for the gift of your Holy Spirit,
who brings us new life in Christ.
Thanks be to you, O God;
you give us the victory through our Lord Jesus Christ. **Amen.**

Prayer of Dedication

God of all glory and grace,
we offer our gifts and our lives to you
in the name of your Son, Jesus Christ,
who gave his life for us,
whom you raised from the dead,
and who lives and reigns with you and the Holy Spirit,
one God for ever and ever. **Amen.**

SECOND SUNDAY OF EASTER

Opening Sentences

Alleluia! Christ is risen!
He is risen indeed! Alleluia!

Prayer of Adoration

'Let everything that has breath praise the Lord!'

Living God,
in your presence there is fullness of joy.
Our hearts are glad and our souls rejoice,
for you show us the path of life.
We worship you for your surpassing greatness;
we adore you for your unconquered love;
in the name of Jesus Christ, our risen Lord. **Amen.**

Prayer of Confession

Forgive us, Lord Jesus,
that, like your first disciples,
we have so little faith,
we harbour many doubts,
we hide away in fear.

Grant us the gift of the Holy Spirit,
revealer of all truth,
that our fears may be overcome,
our doubts resolved,
and our faith quickened;
and that we may live in the power of your resurrection.
We ask it for your name's sake. **Amen.**

Prayer of Thanksgiving

Blessèd are you, the God and Father of our Lord Jesus Christ,
because in your great mercy
you have given us a new birth into a living hope
through the resurrection of Jesus Christ from the dead.

You created us, and all things,
and when we fell into sin,
you sent your Son to be our Saviour.
He took upon him our human nature
and lived our human life,
He died on the Cross for the world's salvation,
but the stone that the builders rejected
has become the cornerstone,
for you raised him to life,
the firstborn of the dead,
to reign with you in glory
and to be the Church's living head.

Through your Holy Spirit,
you have gathered us into Christ's body
to offer you praise and honour
and witness to Christ's gospel
throughout the world.

To him who has loved us
and freed us from our sins –
to him, with you, Father, and the Holy Spirit,
be glory and dominion for ever and ever. **Amen.**

Prayer of Dedication

God of all grace,
we are yours,
created and redeemed by you.
Grant that our words and deeds
may bear witness to Christ's saving work
and the power of his resurrection.
For his sake we ask it. **Amen.**

THIRD SUNDAY OF EASTER

Opening Sentences

Alleluia! Christ is risen!
He is risen indeed! Alleluia!

Prayer of Adoration

Living God,
the God of our ancestors,
the God of Abraham, Isaac and Jacob,
the God of Sarah, Rebekah and Rachel,
the God and Father of our Lord Jesus Christ,
eternal glory is yours and you are worthy of all praise.
In grace and love
you gave your Son to be our Saviour,
to die on the Cross
and to be raised again by you.
To you, seated on the throne of your heavenly majesty,
and to the Lamb, who takes away the world's sin,
be blessing and honour and glory and might
for ever and ever. **Amen.**

Prayer of Confession

Be gracious to us, loving God,
and listen to our prayer.
Forgive us for the many times
when our deeds have belied our words.
Like Peter, we have boasted our allegiance
and then denied our Lord.
We have failed in humble service,
we have failed in trust and obedience,
we have failed in love and forgiveness.
As your Son forgave Peter
and called him to shepherd his sheep,
graciously forgive and renew us
and recall us to your service.
We ask it in his name. **Amen.**

Prayer of Thanksgiving

We give you thanks, eternal God,
for creating the universe
and sustaining it by your power.
We give thanks for your love for us,
your rebellious creatures,
for whom the holy and righteous one,
the author of life,
our Saviour Jesus Christ,
shed his precious blood.
You raised him from the dead
and exalted him in glory,
and through him we have come to trust in you.
In your abundant love,
by the power of the Spirit,
you adopt us as your children
and honour us with the commission
to serve you in the Church and in the world.
Receive this act of thanksgiving,
and grant that our lives may be worthy of our calling;
through Jesus Christ our Lord. **Amen.**

Prayer of Dedication (based on a hymn by Charles Wesley)

Claim us for your service, O God,
and use all that we have and are –
our memories, minds and wills,
our time and our possessions,
our knowledge and our feelings,
our words and thoughts and actions –
to your glory and praise;
through Jesus Christ our Lord. **Amen.**

FOURTH SUNDAY OF EASTER

Opening Sentences

Alleluia! Christ is risen!
He is risen indeed! Alleluia!

Prayer of Adoration

Glory to God, Father, Son and Holy Spirit.

Glory to God the Father,
whose goodness and mercy have followed us
all the days of our life.

Glory to God the Son,
the Good Shepherd, who knows his sheep by name,
and laid down his life for them.

Glory to God the Spirit,
who guides us in the way of Christ
and gathers us into his Church.

Glory to God, Father, Son and Holy Spirit. **Amen.**

Prayer of Confession

God, our Shepherd,
you alone make us dwell in safety.
Yet, like lost sheep,
we have wandered from your ways.
We have failed to hear your voice.
We have tried to live without you.

Pardon our wilful disobedience,
our arrogance and pride;
restore our souls
and lead us in right paths
for your name's sake;
through Jesus Christ our Lord. **Amen.**

Prayer of Thanksgiving

Blessing and glory and wisdom and thanksgiving
and honour and power and might
be to our God for ever and ever!

Glorious and generous God,
the source of all life and love,
we rejoice in the world you created
and give thanks for the gift of life.

We give thanks for your grace and truth,
made known in Jesus Christ,
who suffered for us and laid down his life,
bearing our sins,
that we might live for righteousness;
his wounds have made us whole.

We give you thanks for his resurrection from the dead
and his ascension to your right hand;
for the gift of the Holy Spirit
and our place within the Church.

We give thanks for the lives of your saints,
who faithfully served you on earth.
Christ has guided them to springs of living water
and you have wiped away every tear from their eyes.

Glorious and generous God,
the source of all life and love,
we give thanks for all your goodness,
and we bless your holy name;
through Jesus Christ our Lord. **Amen.**

Prayer of Dedication

God of our salvation,
to whom we owe more than we know
and more than we can repay,
accept the gifts which we offer in love
and our lives devoted to your service,
in the name of Jesus Christ our Lord. **Amen.**

FIFTH SUNDAY OF EASTER

Opening Sentences

Alleluia! Christ is risen!
He is risen indeed! Alleluia!

Prayer of Approach and Adoration

All you angels in heaven,
praise the Lord!
Sun, moon and stars,
praise the Lord!
Fire and hail, wind and snow,
praise the Lord!
Mountains and hills,
praise the Lord!
Wild beasts and cattle,
praise the Lord!
Young and old together,
praise the Lord!
Let all creation
praise the Lord! Amen.

Prayer of Confession

God of love,
you have commanded us to love you with our whole being
and to love one another.

We confess that we have turned away from you,
with cold and indifferent hearts.
We have wandered from your ways
and ignored your Spirit's voice.

We confess that we have not loved one another
as Christ has loved us.
We have seen our brothers and sisters in need
and yet refused to help.
We have compromised with injustice
and failed to act with kindness.

God of love,
forgive our failure to love.

Make your face to shine upon us,
and in your loving-kindness save us;
through Jesus Christ our Lord. **Amen.**

Prayer of Thanksgiving

Eternal God,
Alpha and Omega,
the beginning and the end,
we give you thanks.
You created the heavens and the earth
and made us for yourself.
While we were sinners,
you revealed your love by sending your only Son
that we might live through him.
He is the Way and the Truth and the Life,
who died on the Cross
and was raised by your power
to bring salvation to the world.
Through him, rejected by mortals,
yet chosen and precious in your sight,
you have made us a royal priesthood
to offer you spiritual sacrifices
and to proclaim your mighty acts.
You have called us out of darkness
into your marvellous light
and set before us a glorious hope
of a new heaven and a new earth
where death will be no more
and all the families of the nations will worship you,
eternal God,
in the unity of the Spirit;
through Jesus Christ our Lord. **Amen.**

Prayer of Dedication

God of truth,
our tower, our strength,
the rock of our salvation,
into your hands we commit our lives,
and offer them to your praise;
through Jesus Christ our Lord. **Amen.**

SIXTH SUNDAY OF EASTER

Opening Sentences

Alleluia! The Lord reigns! Let the earth rejoice! Alleluia!

Prayer of Adoration

O God, you are Lord of heaven and earth;
you made the world and everything in it.
Let the peoples praise you, O God.
Let all the peoples praise you.

You give to all mortals life and breath;
in you we live and move and have our being.
Let the peoples praise you, O God.
Let all the peoples praise you.

May all the earth rejoice in you,
breaking forth into joyous songs of praise.
Let the peoples praise you, O God.
Let all the peoples praise you;

through Jesus Christ our Lord. **Amen.**

Prayer of Confession

Jesus said: 'If you love me, you will keep my commandments.'

'Do not store up treasures on earth.'
We confess our love of possessions.

'Do not worry about your life.'
We confess our lack of trust.

'Do not judge, so that you may not be judged.'
We confess our readiness to condemn.

'Be merciful, as your Father is merciful.'
We confess our reluctance to forgive.

'Love your enemies; do good to those that hate you.'
We confess our longing for revenge.

'Do to others as you would have them do to you.'
We confess our slowness to do good.

Merciful God, forgive us these and all our sins;
teach us again the way of Christ
and help us to bear witness to him in deed as in word.
We ask it for his sake. **Amen.**

Prayer of Thanksgiving

It is right and good, most gracious God,
it is our duty and our joy to give you thanks and praise.
In tender care you made the world and you nourish it with love.
To bring us sinners back to you,
you sent your only Son
to share our life and die our death, and be raised again in glory.
He has gone into heaven and reigns at your right hand,
with angels, authorities and powers made subject to him,
and he will judge the world in truth and righteousness.
In the name of Christ you have sent your Spirit, the Advocate,
to be with us for ever, teaching us all things,
reminding us of all that Christ has said to us.
By the leading of the Spirit,
you guide us to that eternal City,
which has no need of sun and moon, for your glory is its light,
and where, with all your people, we shall dwell with you for ever.
For all your love, for all your gifts,
most gracious God, we give you thanks; we bless your holy name;
through Jesus Christ our Lord. **Amen.**

Prayer of Dedication

God of grace and mercy,
thankful for all your love,
we bring our gifts and offer ourselves
to follow Christ and obey his commandments,
who gave his life for us
and lives and reigns, with you and the Spirit,
one God, now and for ever. **Amen.**

ASCENSION DAY

Opening Sentences

Alleluia! The Lord reigns! Let the earth rejoice! Alleluia!

Prayer of Adoration

God, the most high,
more majestic than the thunders of mighty waters,
to you be all glory and praise.
Your Son, our Saviour,
reigns with you in heaven,
the Man of Love, the Crucified,
risen, ascended and glorious.
Through the life-giving Spirit
we bless and adore you.
God, the most high,
through Christ our Lord,
to you be all glory and praise. **Amen.**

Prayer of Confession

Forgive us, Father of glory,
the narrowness of our vision,
our preoccupation with immediate needs,
and our feeble sense of things eternal.
Renew us by your Spirit,
lift our eyes to heaven,
and help us to glimpse Jesus,
our Saviour and our Lord,
who lives and reigns with you and the Spirit,
one God for ever and ever. **Amen.**

Prayer of Thanksgiving

Eternal God,
highly exalted and robed in majesty,
you have established the world,
so that it shall not be moved.
We give you thanks and praise.
We bless your holy name.

You gave your only Son,
who lived and died among us
to bring healing and salvation.
You raised him from the dead
and seated him at your right hand in heaven,
above all powers and authorities,
above every name that is named,
now and for ever.
We give you thanks and praise.
We bless your holy name.

Before he was taken up to heaven
he promised his disciples
that the power of the Holy Spirit would come upon them
so that they might be his witnesses
to the ends of the earth.
We give you thanks and praise.
We bless your holy name.

By the promptings of the same Spirit,
you call us to witness and service
and inspire us to proclaim the gospel
by what we say and do.
For the immeasurable greatness of your power and love,
we give you thanks and praise.
We bless your holy name;
through Jesus Christ our Lord. **Amen.**

Prayer of Dedication

Gracious God,
whose Son Jesus Christ
reigns with you in glory
yet constantly prays for us,
accept the gifts we offer
and our lives dedicated to your service,
and bring us with your saints
to the peace and joy of heaven;
through Jesus Christ our Lord. **Amen.**

SEVENTH SUNDAY OF EASTER

Opening Sentences

Alleluia! The Lord reigns! Let the earth rejoice! Alleluia!

Prayer of Adoration

God, most high over all the earth,
to you be all praise for ever!
God, who gave us eternal life in your Son,
to you be all praise for ever!
God, who called us to eternal glory in Christ,
to you be all praise for ever!
God of power and truth and grace,
to you be all praise for ever;
through Jesus Christ our Lord. **Amen.**

Prayer of Confession

Holy God,
your Son our Saviour prayed for his disciples
that they might be one,
as you and he are one.
We confess our divisions and dissensions
and the disunity we have created
within the Body of Christ.
We have not loved one another
as Christ has loved us.
We have not put past wrongs behind us
or sought reconciliation and healing.
Forgive our sinful thoughts and actions;
help us to start anew;
and sanctify us in the truth of your Word,
our Saviour Jesus Christ. **Amen.**

Prayer of Thanksgiving

In your presence, God of grace,
we are jubilant with joy.
We celebrate your marvellous deeds;
we give you thanks and praise.

For us and for our salvation
you gave your Son,
whom you loved before the world's foundation.
The Alpha and the Omega, the first and the last,
the bright morning star,
he glorified you on earth
by finishing the work which you gave him to do
and dying on the Cross.
You restored him to life
exalting him in glory,
and fulfilled his promise to his disciples
that they would receive power
when the Holy Spirit came upon them.
The Spirit's gifts equip the Church
to preach the gospel in words of power
and acts of humble service.

God of grace,
we celebrate your marvellous deeds;
we give you thanks and praise;
through Jesus Christ our Lord. **Amen.**

Prayer of Dedication

God, the source of all that is good,
you give power and strength to your people.
Thankful for all your mercies,
we present our gifts and our lives,
praying that they may be used,
not for our glory,
but for yours;
for the sake of Christ our Lord. **Amen.**

PENTECOST

Opening Sentence

I will pour out my Spirit on all flesh, says God, and everyone who calls on the name of the Lord shall be saved.

Prayer of Approach and Adoration (based on a hymn by Isaac Watts)

Gracious and Holy Spirit of God,
come to us now
and kindle a flame of love in our cold hearts.
Breathe your life and power into our formal worship
that in spirit and in truth
we may glorify the Father,
in the love of Christ the Son;
for whose sake we ask it. **Amen.**

Prayer of Confession

Merciful God,
whose Spirit bears witness with our spirits
that we are your children,
forgive our many sins.

You have given us the Spirit of truth,
  but we have been deceitful.
You have given us the Spirit of wisdom,
  but we have been foolish.
You have given us the Spirit of discernment,
  but we have made wrong choices.
You have given us the Spirit of patience,
  but we have been impetuous.
You have given us the Spirit of gentleness,
  but we have been unkind.

Forgive us, merciful God.
Make us responsive to the promptings of your Spirit,
and breathe new life into us;
through Jesus Christ our Lord. **Amen.**

Prayer of Thanksgiving

In the beginning, eternal God,
your Spirit brooded over the waters,
creating order out of chaos.
How wonderful are your works; in wisdom you made them all.
The earth is full of your creatures.
When you send forth your Spirit they are brought to birth;
you renew the face of the earth.

We thank you for the Spirit,
by whom Jesus was anointed at his baptism
and revealed as your belovèd Son.
Empowered by the Spirit, he went about doing good
and died for all upon the Cross.
You have raised him again in glory
and sent the Holy Spirit
to help us in our weakness
and intercede for us with sighs too deep for words.

We thank you that, in the one Spirit,
we have been baptized into Christ's Body,
on which the Spirit bestows varied gifts for ministry and mission
as he leads us into the truth.

For the tireless work of your Spirit,
and for all your marvellous deeds,
we praise you and we thank you,
in the name of Jesus Christ our Lord. **Amen.**

Prayer of Dedication

Lead us, Holy Spirit,
  that we may find the way.
Teach us, Holy Spirit,
  that we may know the truth.
Enliven us, Holy Spirit,
  that we may live for Christ.
We ask it in his name
  and for his sake. **Amen.**

TRINITY SUNDAY

Opening Sentence

Holy, holy, holy is the Lord of hosts; the whole earth is full of his glory.

Prayer of Adoration

Sovereign God,
how majestic is your name in all the earth!
You have set your glory above the heavens.
We worship you in your holy splendour.
When we look up and see the sky,
the moon and stars which you have established,
we wonder that you should care for us, mere mortals.
Yet you have made us a little lower than yourself
and crowned us with glory and honour.
Sovereign God,
how majestic is your name in all the earth!
We worship you in your holy splendour;
through Jesus Christ our Lord. **Amen.**

Prayer of Confession

You are holy, eternal God,
but we are sinners in need of forgiveness.
You are gracious, eternal God,
but we are jealous and proud.
You are righteous, eternal God,
but we are unjust and uncaring.
You are faithful, eternal God,
but we are false and unreliable.
You are loving, eternal God,
but we are selfish and unkind.
For the sake of your Son,
eternal God, forgive us.
Restore your image within us,
and strengthen us by your Spirit;
through our Saviour Jesus Christ. **Amen.**

Prayer of Thanksgiving

Mighty and gracious God,
to you be all thanks and praise.
You created the universe by your powerful word
and saw that it was good.
You made humankind in your image
and gave your Son for our redemption.
In his life and death and resurrection
we discover your loving purpose.
Through him we have been born anew,
of water and the Spirit;
through him we have peace with you
and rejoice in the hope of sharing your glory
as joint heirs with Christ our Saviour.
By the Holy Spirit, given to us,
your love has been poured into our hearts.

Mighty and gracious God,
to you be all thanks and praise.
Your Spirit dwells within us,
revealing the truth of Christ
and strengthening us to proclaim the gospel,
teaching, baptizing and making disciples,
in every nation.

Mighty and gracious God,
to you be all thanks and praise,
with Jesus Christ our Saviour
and the Spirit of truth and love,
now and for ever. **Amen.**

Prayer of Dedication (based on a hymn by Charles Wesley)

Father, Son and Holy Spirit,
One-in-Three and Three-in-One,
we offer ourselves to you.
Sanctify all that we think and say and do;
use in your service all that we have and are,
and grant that we may live to your glory. **Amen.**

SUNDAY BETWEEN 24 AND 28 MAY

Eighth Sunday in Ordinary Time

Opening Sentences

Sing for joy, O heavens, and exult, O earth. For the Lord has comforted his people.

Prayer of Approach

As we come into your presence,
God of our salvation,
help us to calm and quieten our spirits.
Open our eyes, that we may catch sight of your glory.
Open our ears, that we may hear your word.
Open our hearts, that we may respond in love;
through Jesus Christ our Lord. **Amen.**

Prayer of Confession

Compassionate God,
your Son Jesus Christ came to call
not the righteous, but sinners.
We confess that we are sinners
and we seek your forgiveness
for the times when we have called Jesus 'Lord'
but not done what he commands;
for the times when we have seen the speck in another's eye
but been blind to the log in our own;
for the times when we have been slow to forgive
but quick to take offence.
In steadfast love and mercy,
listen to our prayer.
Pardon our transgressions
and strengthen us by your Spirit.
We ask it for Christ's sake. **Amen.**

Prayer of Thanksgiving

'Bless the Lord, O my soul; and all that is within me, bless his holy name.'

It is good to give thanks to you, O God,
to praise your name, O Most High.
You created the heavens and the earth
and saw that they were good.
You made us for yourself
and when, in our folly and disobedience,
we turned away from you,
you did not abandon us
but sought us in your love.

We give you thanks for the victory
which you give us in the Lord Jesus Christ;
for in his life and death and resurrection
he has conquered sin and death for us,
and through our baptism we share in his risen life.

We thank you for our place within the Church,
for nourishment in word and sacrament,
and for our calling to be servants of Christ
and stewards of your mysteries,
with your Spirit at work within us,
moving us to worship and witness.
All praise and thanks be given to you,
through Jesus Christ your Son,
in the unity of the Holy Spirit
now and for ever. **Amen.**

Prayer of Dedication

Giving thanks for all your goodness,
we bring our gifts to you, O God,
and offer ourselves in your service.
Help us to be faithful and fruitful in this life
and, by your mercy,
bring us with your saints
to your eternal kingdom;
through Jesus Christ our Lord. **Amen.**

SUNDAY BETWEEN 29 MAY AND 4 JUNE

Ninth Sunday in Ordinary Time

Opening Sentence

Grace to you and peace from God our Father and the Lord Jesus Christ.

Prayer of Approach and Adoration

Everlasting God,
there is no God like you
in heaven above or on earth beneath,
keeping covenant in steadfast love
with your servants.
You are faithful and true,
our rock and our fortress.
You are great, and greatly to be praised.
As we come into your presence,
accept our worship
and hear our prayers;
for we offer them in the name of Jesus Christ our Lord. **Amen.**

Prayer of Confession

God of compassion,
hear us from heaven
and forgive our sins.
We acknowledge with penitence
that we have broken your commandments;
we have sinned and fallen short of your glory.
In words and in actions,
in heart and in mind,
we have gone astray.
Have mercy upon us,
deliver us from our sins,
and wash away all our guilt;
for the sake of your Son our Saviour. **Amen.**

Prayer of Thanksgiving

Blessèd are you, eternal God,
ever to be trusted,
giver of life and creator of the universe.
You led your people out of Egypt
with a mighty hand and an outstretched arm,
and you delivered the world from sin and death
in Jesus Christ your Son.
Born of Mary,
he shared our human life,
proclaiming your kingdom,
teaching with authority,
and healing the sick, in body and mind.
Despised and rejected, he died on the Cross,
but you raised him to life
and restored him to your right hand.
We give thanks that in his face
we have seen the light of your glory,
that through him we are justified by your grace,
and that, guided and led by your Spirit,
we are called to spread Christ's reconciling love
wherever we may go.

Blessèd are you, eternal God;
to you be all glory and praise,
now and for ever;
through Jesus Christ our Lord. **Amen.**

Prayer of Dedication

We are yours, most holy God,
made and redeemed by your love.
Help us to give ourselves to you without reserve.
May your law be written in our hearts
that we may both hear your words and act on them;
and to you be all glory and honour
in time and in eternity;
through Jesus Christ our Lord. **Amen.**

SUNDAY BETWEEN 5 AND 11 JUNE

Tenth Sunday in Ordinary Time

Opening Sentence

God, who raised the Lord Jesus, will raise us also with Jesus, and will bring us into his presence.

Prayer of Approach

Eternal God,
the birth of whose Son
was heralded by the song of the angels,
and whom the hosts of heaven worship night and day,
assist us by your Holy Spirit
that we may worthily sing your praises
and worship you with reverence and joy;
through Jesus Christ our Lord. **Amen.**

Prayer of Confession

'Come, let us return to the Lord.'

Your love for us, O God, is constant,
steadfast and consistent.
Our love for you is fickle;
it evaporates like morning dew.
Your love for us is costly;
you gave your only Son for our salvation.
Our love for you is limited;
we flinch from any sacrifice.
Your love for us is beyond understanding;
we know that we do not deserve it.
Our love for you is feeble and weak;
you deserve wholehearted devotion.

In love and mercy, forgive us;
and teach us to love you
with all our heart, soul, mind and strength,
and our neighbours as ourselves;
through Jesus Christ our Lord. **Amen.**

Prayer of Thanksgiving

God of love,
the whole creation resounds to your glory,
for you are its maker
and you hold it in being.
We give you blessing and thanks.

For the sake of lost sinners,
Jesus Christ your Son lived among us.
We thank you that he did not stand aloof
from those whom others despised,
but ate with tax-collectors and sinners,
calling them to repentance.
He healed the sick and gave sight to the blind;
he made lepers clean and lame people walk.
We thank you that, even on the Cross,
he forgave those who were his enemies.
Raised to life for our justification,
he lives with you in glory,
praying for us constantly
and empowering us through his Spirit.
God of love, creator and redeemer,
we give you blessing and thanks
now and for ever;
in the name of Jesus our Lord. **Amen.**

Prayer of Dedication

We offer to you, living God,
all that we have and are,
in the name of him who lived and died
and was raised from death
for the sake of all the world,
our Lord and Saviour, Jesus Christ. **Amen.**

SUNDAY BETWEEN 12 AND 18 JUNE

Eleventh Sunday in Ordinary Time

Opening Sentence

Worship the Lord with gladness, and come into his presence with singing.

Prayer of Approach and Adoration

Eternal God,
you are the one who made us
and we are yours.
We are your people,
the sheep of your pasture.
We enter your house with thanksgiving;
we come to this place with praise.
All honour and glory be yours,
in time and in eternity;
through Jesus Christ our Lord. **Amen.**

Prayer of Confession

Merciful God,
the praise we seek to offer
is spoilt by our failure to do your will.
We have despised your holy word
and done what is evil in your sight.
We have professed to follow Christ
but we have not shown his humble love
or borne the burdens of others.
We acknowledge our many sins
and repent with all our hearts.
Speak to us now,
as your Son once spoke to a sinful woman,
and say to each of us
'Your sins are forgiven; go in peace';
through Jesus Christ our Lord. **Amen.**

Prayer of Thanksgiving

God of all goodness and grace,
the whole earth is yours,
created and sustained by your power.
Your steadfast love endures for ever,
your faithfulness to all generations.

We bless you and give thanks to you
for Jesus Christ your Son.
He showed your grace and love
and declared your forgiveness to penitent sinners.
Your steadfast love endures for ever,
your faithfulness to all generations.

We thank you that, while we were still weak,
Christ died for the ungodly,
and that you raised him from the dead
to live and reign in glory.
Your steadfast love endures for ever,
your faithfulness to all generations.

We thank you that we are justified, not by our own deeds,
but through faith in Jesus Christ,
in whom we are a new creation.
Your steadfast love endures for ever,
your faithfulness to all generations.

We thank you for the Holy Spirit,
and for your Church, on earth and in heaven,
witnessing to your truth and glorifying your name.
Your steadfast love endures for ever,
your faithfulness to all generations;
through Jesus Christ our Lord. **Amen.**

Prayer of Dedication

May our gifts, God of grace,
be signs of our dedication of ourselves;
and may we live, no longer for ourselves,
but for him who died and was raised for us,
our Saviour Jesus Christ. **Amen.**

SUNDAY BETWEEN 19 AND 25 JUNE

Twelfth Sunday in Ordinary Time

Opening Sentence

All the ends of the earth shall remember and turn to the Lord; and all the families of the nations shall worship before him.

Prayer of Adoration

God of strength and wisdom,
high and exalted above all,
yet closer to us than breathing,
you are worthy of all praise.
You created the galaxies, the planets and this earth.
You made us for yourself
and have given us wills with which to obey you
and voices to sing your praise.
May we find life's true purpose in doing your will
and joining the whole creation
in adoring your holy name;
through Jesus Christ our Lord. **Amen.**

Prayer of Confession

God all-seeing,
you read our hearts and minds
and we have no secrets from you.
We confess that we hide the truth from others
and try to hide it from ourselves.
But you know what we are –
sinners who have strayed from your paths
and followed our own devices.
In your abundant, steadfast love,
listen to our prayer.
Forgive what we have been and done;
help us to change our ways;
and bring us, with your saints,
to everlasting glory;
through the merits of Jesus Christ our Saviour. **Amen.**

Prayer of Thanksgiving

God, who laid the foundations of the earth
and divided sea from land,
we rejoice in your creative might
and your wonderful works to humankind.
Despite our wilful disobedience,
you came to us in Jesus.
He proclaimed your kingdom
in powerful words
and acts of compassion and love.
Lifted on the shameful Cross,
he transformed its shame to glory.
You raised him to live for ever,
for death has no more dominion over him.
Buried with him in baptism,
we have been raised up to walk in newness of life
and adopted as your children
within that family
which knows no distinctions of status or race,
for all are one in Christ Jesus.

We thank you for all faithful Christians
who, by their lives and their deaths,
have witnessed to Christ's gospel;
and we pray that our thankfulness
may be expressed, not only in prayer,
but by the way we live our lives;
through Jesus Christ our Lord. **Amen.**

Prayer of Dedication

Your generous gifts to us, O God,
are more than we can count.
With grateful hearts
we dedicate to you
our work, our talents, our time,
and pray that you will use us
in the service of your kingdom;
for the sake of Christ our Saviour. **Amen.**

SUNDAY BETWEEN 26 JUNE AND 2 JULY

Thirteenth Sunday in Ordinary Time

Opening Sentences

God's steadfast love is established for ever. God's faithfulness is as firm as the heavens.

Prayer of Approach and Adoration

Lord God,
your steadfast love never ceases,
your mercies never come to an end;
they are new every morning.
Great is your faithfulness.
You show us the path of life
and in your presence
there is fullness of joy.
Accept this act of worship
and use it for your glory;
through Jesus Christ our Lord. **Amen.**

Prayer of Confession

Generous God,
you have poured out your Spirit on the Church,
but we have resisted the Spirit's work within us.

The fruit of the Spirit is love and joy,
  but we have been cold and gloomy.
The fruit of the Spirit is peace and patience,
  but we have been restless and agitated.
The fruit of the Spirit is kindness and generosity,
  but we have been thoughtless and mean.
The fruit of the Spirit is faithfulness and gentleness,
  but we have been fickle and harsh.
The fruit of the Spirit is self-control,
  but we have been undisciplined.

Forgive us, O God,
and guide us by your Spirit;
for the sake of Christ our Saviour. **Amen.**

Prayer of Thanksgiving

Most loving God,
creator of all that is good,
we bless your holy name.

Through Jesus Christ
you have revealed that your purposes for the world
are those of grace and love.
His ministry and death and rising
make plain your will
that all should have fullness of life.
Though what we sinners deserve is death,
you freely give us eternal life
in Jesus Christ our Lord.

We bless you for the Holy Spirit,
whose gifts build up the Church
and equip us to serve the world in love
and proclaim the good news of Christ.

Most loving God,
we bless your holy name,
and worship you, with the Son and the Spirit;
now and for ever. **Amen.**

Prayer of Dedication

Eternal God,
your Son Jesus Christ was rich,
yet for our sake he became poor,
that we, through his poverty, might become rich.
Accept the gifts which we offer
as symbols of our love
and of our lives dedicated to your service.
We ask it for his sake. **Amen.**

SUNDAY BETWEEN 3 AND 9 JULY

Fourteenth Sunday in Ordinary Time

Opening Sentences

God's kingdom is an everlasting kingdom, and his dominion endures throughout all generations.

Prayer of Adoration

You are enthroned above the heavens, O God,
and we lift up our eyes to you.
The wonder of your being surpasses human thought,
for you are perfect in wisdom, holiness and might,
yet gracious and merciful,
slow to anger and abounding in love,
though we have sinned against you.
As a mother comforts her child,
so you comfort us.
You are the ground of our being,
the source of our life,
the foundation of our hope,
and we worship you with jubilant praise;
in the name of Jesus Christ our Lord. **Amen.**

Prayer of Confession

God, most merciful and most holy,
we confess our deliberate sins.
We have been rebellious and stubborn,
determined to please ourselves,
disobedient to your call.
And we confess our unintended sins,
when we will to do what is right,
but fail to do it,
and do what is evil instead.
Have mercy upon us, gracious God.
Deliver us from sin and from self,
and strengthen us by your Spirit
that we may delight in your law

and walk in your way;
through Jesus Christ our Lord. **Amen.**

Prayer of Thanksgiving

All your works give thanks to you, O God,
and all your people bless you.
We recount with joy your marvellous deeds
and celebrate your goodness.
We thank you for Jesus, our Saviour and Lord,
your belovèd and only Son,
who came to this earth to bring healing and hope
and to shine as a light in our darkness.
In his life and his death
he has taught us the truth
that when we are weak, then we are strong,
for your grace is sufficient for all our needs.
We rejoice that Jesus, in triumph and victory,
was gentle and humble in heart,
and that, raised to eternal glory,
he understands our frailty
and prays for us for ever.
By the gracious work of your Spirit,
you guide us in witness and service
and lead us to our promised land
in your eternal kingdom.
For all your great and wonderful deeds
we bless your holy name;
in Jesus Christ our Lord. **Amen.**

Prayer of Dedication (based on a hymn by Charles Wesley)

Lord Jesus Christ,
we long to find in ourselves
a passion like yours for the Father
and a love like yours for humankind.
May your Spirit dwell within us,
and your compassion move in our hearts,
that the driving force of our being
may be the pure flame of your love.
We ask it in your name and for your sake. **Amen.**

SUNDAY BETWEEN 10 AND 16 JULY

Fifteenth Sunday in Ordinary Time

Opening Sentence

God has rescued us from the power of darkness and transferred us into the kingdom of his belovèd Son, in whom we have redemption, the forgiveness of our sins.

Prayer of Approach and Adoration

We come with reverence to your house, O God;
we come in humility to this holy place.
For you are glorious and exalted,
holy and righteous and good,
and we are weak and sinful,
unworthy to stand before you.
Yet in your grace and mercy,
you have bridged the gap between earth and heaven,
stretching your hand out to us in Jesus Christ your Son.
And so we come, humbly and reverently,
but also secure in your love,
and we offer you praise and honour,
in the saving name of Jesus. **Amen.**

Prayer of Confession

Let us in silence call to mind our sins.

Silence

For our pride and self-assertion,
merciful God, forgive us.

For our folly and complacency,
merciful God, forgive us.

For our anger and aggression,
merciful God, forgive us.

For our jealousy and envy,
merciful God, forgive us.

For our taintedness and impurity,
merciful God, forgive us.

To those who are penitent Jesus says: Your sins are forgiven.
Thanks be to God. **Amen.**

Prayer of Thanksgiving

Eternal God,
you spoke the universe into being
and your word succeeds in the purposes for which you send it.
It is not far from us, but very near, implanted deep within us.
We thank you, eternal God.

Eternal Son,
Word of the Father,
you took our human flesh and spoke to us the word of life.
Your Cross and resurrection
proclaim undying love for the world
and in you we are called to share in the heritage of the saints in light.
We thank you, eternal Son.

Eternal Spirit,
in whom is life and peace,
your voice invites us to bear fruit in every good work
and to grow in knowledge and grace.
You are our guide and inspiration, our advocate and strength.
We thank you, eternal Spirit.

Glory to the Father and to the Son and to the Holy Spirit;
as it was in the beginning, is now and shall be for ever. **Amen.**

Prayer of Dedication

God and Father of Jesus,
you destined us for adoption as your children
and in Christ have abundantly blessed us.
We give you these gifts,
and with them our lives,
to the glory of your name;
through Jesus Christ our Lord. **Amen.**

SUNDAY BETWEEN 17 AND 23 JULY

Sixteenth Sunday in Ordinary Time

Opening Sentence

Through Christ, God was pleased to reconcile to himself all things, whether on earth or in heaven, by making peace through his blood which was shed on the Cross.

Prayer of Approach

God eternal,
we come into your presence,
worried and distracted by many things.
Calm our thoughts and our hearts;
help us to fix our minds on you;
and assist us by your Spirit;
that we may praise and worship you aright;
for the sake of Jesus Christ our Lord. **Amen.**

Prayer of Confession

Have mercy upon us, O God,
for we are sinners.
Impure in heart and mean of spirit,
careless of others and deaf to your voice,
we have lived for ourselves
and neglected our calling.
Yet you are gracious and full of compassion,
abounding in kindness and forbearance.
Forgive our sins,
and teach us your way,
that we may walk in your truth
and give glory to you;
through Jesus Christ our Lord. **Amen.**

Prayer of Thanksgiving

Righteous God,
the first and the last,
we thank you with all our heart.
For great is your love for the world you have made,
and great is your love for us.
To redeem lost sinners,
you gave your Son, Jesus Christ,
the firstborn of all creation,
in whom all things were made.
He lived on this earth
and proclaimed your kingdom.
He healed the sick
and sowed seeds of truth.
Through his death on the Cross
and his glorious resurrection,
you have reconciled all things to yourself
and through him you have made us
members of your household,
built on the foundation of the apostles and prophets,
with Christ himself as the cornerstone.
You have sent us your Spirit
to bear witness with our spirits
that we are your children,
to prompt our prayers
and to guide us in service and mission.
For all these acts of grace and love,
we offer thanks and praise;
in the name of Christ our Saviour. **Amen.**

Prayer of Dedication

Lord Jesus, we are yours;
we acknowledge your authority,
and dedicate our lives to you.
Teach us, like Martha,
to be busy in your service,
and, like Mary,
to sit at your feet and listen to your voice,
that our whole being may be offered to you.
We ask it for your sake. **Amen.**

SUNDAY BETWEEN 24 AND 30 JULY

Seventeenth Sunday in Ordinary Time

Opening Sentences

The Lord is faithful in all his words and gracious in all his deeds.
The Lord is just in all his ways and kind in all his doings.

Prayer of Approach and Adoration

God of grace and glory,
ever worthy of worship,
you are near to all who call upon you.
As we worship you in your glorious majesty,
help us to know your presence among us
and to grasp the breadth and length and height and depth
of the love of Christ your Son, our Saviour.
We ask it in his name. **Amen.**

Prayer of Confession

Judge of all the earth,
you do what is right.
But we are sinners,
prone to do what is wrong.

Forgive the selfishness of our actions,
our weak concern for justice,
our misuse and pollution of this planet,
and our lack of care for others.

Pardon our offences
and make your face shine on us
that we may walk before you in faithfulness,
in righteousness and in uprightness of heart;
through Jesus Christ our Lord. **Amen.**

Prayer of Thanksgiving

God of great and steadfast love,
we thank you for your goodness.
You have given us life and you hold us in being.
You are our creator and sustainer.
You keep us in your care.

We thank you that, in Christ your Son,
you rescued us from sin.
He died for us
and you nailed to the Cross
the record that stood against us.
You raised him from death
and you have raised us with him
to live in newness of life.
We bless you that neither death nor life,
nor things present, nor things to come,
nor height nor depth,
nor anything else in all creation,
can separate us from your love
in Jesus Christ our Lord.

We thank you for the Holy Spirit,
giver of life and fire of your love,
who intercedes for all your people
according to your will.

Now to you, O God,
who can accomplish abundantly
far more than we can ask or imagine,
be glory in the Church and in Christ Jesus
to all generations, for ever and ever. **Amen.**

Prayer of Dedication

Father in heaven,
we offer ourselves
in the service of your kingdom.
Strengthen us with power through your Spirit
and grant that as Christ dwells in our hearts by faith
we may be rooted and grounded in love
and, knowing his love
which surpasses knowledge,
may be filled with all your fullness;
through Jesus Christ our Lord. **Amen.**

SUNDAY BETWEEN 31 JULY AND 6 AUGUST

Eighteenth Sunday in Ordinary Time

Opening Sentence

There is one body and one Spirit, one Lord, one faith, one baptism, one God and Father of all, who is above all and through all and in all.

Prayer of Approach and Adoration

God, blessèd for ever,
you uphold those who are falling
and raise up those who are bowed down.
In our weakness and weariness
we come into your house.
Lift our eyes and broaden our horizons
that we may set our minds on the things which are above,
in the peace and joy of your presence,
and worship you with glad and reverent hearts;
through Jesus Christ our Lord. **Amen.**

Prayer of Confession

Eternal God,
whose compassion is over all that you have made,
we need your forgiveness.

We have trusted in our wealth
and boasted of the abundance of our possessions.
We have not put our trust in you, the true and living God.
Lord, have mercy.
Lord, have mercy.

We have longed for ease and comfort
and grown weary of well doing.
We have not sought refreshment from the true and living Bread.
Lord, have mercy.
Lord, have mercy.

We have followed human wisdom
and relied on our own understanding.

We have not sought enlightenment from the true and living Spirit.
Lord, have mercy.
Lord, have mercy.

Here is good news for all who repent. Jesus says: 'Your sins are forgiven.'
Thanks be to God. **Amen.**

Prayer of Thanksgiving

It is right and fitting, holy God,
that we should praise and thank you.
With the whole creation,
which you made in beauty and splendour,
we lift up our hearts and our voices to bless your glorious name.
We thank you for the Church throughout the world
and for the varied gifts which your Spirit gives
to equip us for the work of ministry
and the building up of the Body of Christ.
We thank you for Jesus, the Church's head,
who lived and died and was raised again
for the salvation of humankind.
We thank you for the Spirit of unity,
who draws us together in the one Body
where old distinctions of race or status no longer count
for Christ is all and is in all.
We thank you for the communion of saints,
and the glorious hope of our calling;
and we long for the day when all the earth shall praise your name;
through Jesus Christ our Lord. **Amen.**

Prayer of Dedication (based on a hymn by Charles Wesley)

Being of beings, God of love,
you have made, preserved and saved us.
We long to be wholly yours.
Thankful for all your mercies,
we give ourselves to you.
By your Holy Spirit
fill our hearts with the love of Christ
and help us to do your will;
for the sake of Jesus Christ our Saviour. **Amen.**

SUNDAY BETWEEN 7 AND 13 AUGUST

Nineteenth Sunday in Ordinary Time

Opening Sentence

O magnify the Lord with me and let us exalt his name together.

Prayer of Approach and Adoration

God, our help and our shield,
more powerful than earthquake, wind or fire,
speak to us in the silence
and draw us close to you.

Silence

Heavenly Father, to you be all praise.
Gracious Redeemer, to you be all praise.
Comforting Spirit, to you be all praise;
now and for ever. **Amen.**

Prayer of Confession

Have mercy upon us, O God,
for we have grieved your Holy Spirit.
Forgive our lack of honesty,
our failure to speak the truth.
Pardon our lack of forgiveness,
our anger and our bitterness.
Forgive our lack of compassion,
our slowness to love our neighbour.
Pardon our lack of grace,
our malice and our intolerance.
Help us to love as Christ loved us,
to be kind and tender-hearted,
forgiving one another
as you in Christ have forgiven us.
We ask it in his name and for his sake. **Amen.**

Prayer of Thanksgiving

Our hearts are glad in you, O God;
we rejoice in your mighty acts.
We have tasted and seen that you are good;
we celebrate your kindness.
To save the world from slavery to sin
you sent your only Son.
He gave himself up to death for us,
a fragrant offering and sacrifice to you,
and, in your boundless mercy,
you give eternal life
to all who confess that Jesus is Lord
and believe in their hearts
that you raised him from death.
He is for us the Bread of Life,
our nourishment and strength.
He has prepared a place for us
that we may be with him.
He calls us to a life of faith
and guides us by his Spirit.
He gathers disciples from every land
and makes us members of one another.
He is our treasure and our joy,
our Saviour and our Lord;
and in his name we give you thanks
and rejoice in you for ever. **Amen.**

Prayer of Dedication

You are worthy, generous God,
of more than we can offer,
and even what we have to give
has come to us from you.
Accept our bodies, minds and souls,
our sacrifice of praise,
and use us for your kingdom's sake;
through Jesus Christ our Lord. **Amen.**

SUNDAY BETWEEN 14 AND 20 AUGUST

Twentieth Sunday in Ordinary Time

Opening Sentence

Sing and make melody to the Lord, giving thanks at all times in the name of our Lord Jesus Christ.

Prayer of Adoration

Great you are, eternal God,
deserving of all praise.
Let all the peoples praise you, God.
Let all the peoples praise you.

Great is your glory, eternal God;
you dwell in splendour and light.
Let all the peoples praise you, God.
Let all the peoples praise you.

Great is your power, eternal God,
creator of the universe.
Let all the peoples praise you, God.
Let all the peoples praise you.

Great is your love, eternal God;
you are merciful to all.
Let all the peoples praise you, God.
Let all the peoples praise you;
through Jesus Christ our Lord. **Amen.**

Prayer of Confession

Almighty God, our Maker and Judge,
we have been born into a sinful world
and we ourselves are sinners.
We have sinned against you
and against our neighbours
and fallen short of what you meant us to be.
We have thought too much of ourselves and too little of you.
We have turned aside from the needy
and ignored the weak and the destitute.

Have mercy upon us
and renew us by your Spirit,
that we may depart from evil and do good,
seek peace and pursue it,
and serve you with our whole being;
for the sake of our Saviour Christ. **Amen.**

Prayer of Thanksgiving

We thank you, God most gracious,
for creating the heavens and the earth
and making us in your image.
We thank you that, when we turned from you
in foolish disobedience,
you sought to win us back,
and sent your Son, our Saviour Christ,
to be the pioneer and perfecter of our faith.
He endured the Cross, disregarding its shame,
and has taken his seat at your right hand.
We thank you that, by the power of your Spirit,
you have formed and guided the Church.
We thank you for the long tradition
of Christian worship and service
and for the great cloud of witnesses that surrounds us.
As we thank you for all these mercies,
we pray that your Spirit may lead us
to fulfil our appointed mission
and share in Christ's final victory.
We ask it in the ever-blessèd name
of Jesus Christ our Lord. **Amen.**

Prayer of Dedication

Take our gifts, most loving God,
that they may be used for your glory.
Take our hearts, most loving God,
that they may be filled with love.
Take our wills, most loving God,
that they may be obedient to your call.
Take our actions, most loving God,
that they may bring you praise;
through Jesus Christ our Lord. **Amen.**

SUNDAY BETWEEN 21 AND 27 AUGUST

Twenty-first Sunday in Ordinary Time

Opening Sentence

Bless the Lord, O my soul, who crowns you with steadfast love and mercy.

Prayer of Approach and Adoration

Heaven and earth are full of your glory,
majestic, holy, all-powerful God.
We approach the blazing light of your presence
with reverence and awe, with humility and penitence.
Accept our adoration and teach us through your word
so that, strengthened by your Spirit,
our lives may be lived to your glory;
through Jesus Christ, your Son, in whom we make our prayer. **Amen.**

Prayer of Confession

'Do not think of yourselves more highly than you ought to think.'

Compassionate God, forgive us for thinking
too highly of ourselves in relation to you.
Forgive the pride that makes us imagine that we know what is best,
regardless of your commandments.
Forgive the arrogance that leads us to act
as though the whole world revolved around us.
Forgive the complacency that allows us to be content
with our fainthearted discipleship.
Lord, have mercy.
Lord, have mercy.

Compassionate God, forgive us for thinking
too highly of ourselves in relation to others.
Forgive the selfishness that makes us behave
as though they existed for our benefit.
Forgive the self-righteousness that leads us to judge
sisters and brothers for whom Christ died.
Forgive the self-concern that allows us to ignore the needy
and withhold food from the hungry

Lord, have mercy.
Lord, have mercy.

Compassionate God,
forgive our sins and purify our minds,
that in thought and in action we may be worthy of our calling,
in Jesus Christ our Lord. **Amen.**

Prayer of Thanksgiving

We give you thanks, eternal God, Father, Son and Holy Spirit.

We thank you, God the Father.
You made the universe in beauty and splendour;
you created us, male and female, in your image;
you graciously revealed your loving purposes,
above all in your Son Jesus Christ.
We thank you, God the Father,

We thank you, God the Son.
You came to earth with the words of eternal life.
We thank you for your humble birth,
for your ministry of teaching, preaching and healing,
for your death on the Cross,
for your glorious resurrection and ascension,
for your unceasing intercession for us,
and for the gift of the Holy Spirit.
We thank you, God the Son.

We thank you, God the Holy Spirit,
source of all goodness, beauty and truth.
You are for ever with the people of Jesus,
guiding them, guarding them, leading them into truth;
you inspire and prompt our worship and service.
We thank you, God the Holy Spirit.

We give you thanks, eternal God, Father, Son and Holy Spirit;
now and for ever. **Amen.**

Prayer of Dedication

As we offer our gifts to you, God of love,
we present ourselves as a living sacrifice
and pray that it may be holy and acceptable to you;
for the sake of Jesus Christ our Lord. **Amen.**

SUNDAY BETWEEN 28 AUGUST AND 3 SEPTEMBER

Twenty-second Sunday in Ordinary Time

Opening Sentence

You are worthy, our Lord and God, to receive glory and honour and power.

Prayer of Adoration

Ever-living God,
you are utterly to be trusted.
You are without variation or change.
Your goodness lasts for ever.
Your Son, the Word made flesh,
proclaimed your constancy
by deeds consistent with his words.
He taught us to be humble in spirit –
and lived a life of selfless service,
kneeling to wash his disciples' feet.
He taught us to trust in you and do your will –
and walked the way of obedience and faith,
from the wilderness to Gethsemane,
from Gethsemane to Calvary.
He taught us to love and forgive –
and he loved to the end
and forgave those who nailed him to the Cross.
Ever-living God,
utterly to be trusted,
revealed to us in Jesus,
we worship and adore you in his name. **Amen.**

Prayer of Confession

Gracious God,
forgive us that our deeds so often fail to match our words.
We honour you with our lips
but our hearts are far from you.
We profess to follow Jesus
but we do not live as he taught us to live.
We call him the Pearl of Great Price
but we harbour the love of money.

We claim to care for others
but we hurt them by actions and negligence.
In compassion and grace, forgive us.
Renew us by your Spirit
and make us doers of your word,
for the sake of him who is the same,
yesterday, today and for ever,
our Saviour Jesus Christ. **Amen.**

Prayer of Thanksgiving

We thank you, generous God,
for the beauty of the fruitful earth,
for the love of families and friends,
for the community in which we live
and for the fellowship of the Church.

We thank you for our Lord Jesus Christ,
for his life and his example,
for his death and his resurrection,
and for the commission given to his disciples
to carry on his work
in the power of the Holy Spirit.

We thank you for the gift of faith
and pray that it may find expression in the life of the Church
as we build each other up,
and in the life of the community,
as we encourage the young, cheer the old,
visit the sick and help the needy.
Grant that, by the words we speak and the lives we live,
we may spread Christ's gospel of love and peace.
We ask it in his name. **Amen.**

Prayer of Dedication

To you, O God, we bring these gifts,
and ask you to work in our lives,
that we may rejoice in hope,
being patient in suffering,
hospitable and humble,
living in peace with all,
and serving you with ardent spirits;
through Jesus Christ our Lord. **Amen.**

SUNDAY BETWEEN 4 AND 10 SEPTEMBER

Twenty-third Sunday in Ordinary Time

Opening Sentence

Jesus said: Where two or three are gathered in my name, I am there among them.

Prayer of Approach and Adoration (based on a hymn by Charles Wesley)

God of love,
your grace extends throughout the world,
immense and unconfined,
wide as infinity,
reaching out to all,
reaching out to us.
We come in wonder and praise
to offer you our worship;
in the name of Jesus Christ our Lord. **Amen.**

Prayer of Confession

Most holy God,
we are taught in your word
that love is the fulfilling of the law.
Forgive our failures to love.

Forgive our little love for you,
our waywardness and ingratitude.
We have not loved you with our whole being,
with heart and soul and mind and strength.

Forgive our little love for others,
our selfishness and unkindness.
We have not loved our neighbours as ourselves,
or cared for them as we ought to have cared.

In your love and mercy,
blot out our offences,
and sow in our hearts the seeds of your love

that they may bear abundant fruit;
through Jesus Christ our Lord. **Amen.**

Prayer of Thanksgiving

Living God,
who made heaven and earth,
you gave us life
so that we might love and obey you
and hold fast to you for ever.
When we wandered from your ways,
your Son Jesus Christ came to dwell among us,
bringing healing and salvation.
He made the deaf to hear and the mute to speak;
he opened eyes that were blind
and revealed your loving purposes.
He died on the Cross
and you raised him from the dead,
restoring to him the glory that was his before time began.
In your tender mercy,
you have chosen the poor in the world
to be rich in faith
and heirs of the kingdom
which you have promised to those who love you;
and have poured out your Holy Spirit,
our Advocate and Guide.
For all your mighty acts of grace and love
we give you thanks and praise;
through Jesus Christ our Lord. **Amen.**

Prayer of Dedication

Rejoicing in your goodness, Lord,
we dedicate our lives to you.
Dwell in our hearts,
enlighten our minds,
guide our steps,
and direct our actions,
to the glory of your holy name.
For Christ's sake we ask it. **Amen.**

SUNDAY BETWEEN 11 AND 17 SEPTEMBER

Twenty-fourth Sunday in Ordinary Time

Opening Sentence

As the heavens are high above the earth, so great is God's steadfast love towards those who fear him.

Prayer of Adoration

You are righteous and gracious, O God,
slow to anger and merciful.
You do not deal with us according to our sins,
or repay us according to our evil ways.
You answer our ingratitude with kindness.
Your love for us never fails.
You deserve praise without ceasing
and adoration for ever.
All glory and honour and blessing be yours,
world without end. **Amen.**

Prayer of Confession

Merciful God,
your Son has taught us
that there is more joy in heaven
over one penitent sinner
than over ninety-nine righteous people who need no repentance.
We sinners repent of our sins.

We confess the wrong words we have spoken.
With the same tongues that have blessed your name
we have spoken ill of those made in your likeness.
We confess the wrong thoughts we have entertained.
We have despised and judged our brothers and sisters
and been slow to forgive their behaviour.
We confess the wrong deeds we have done.
We have worshipped the idols of wealth and power
and acted unjustly and selfishly.

We sinners repent of our sins.
We recall with joy that Christ Jesus our Lord
came into the world to save sinners
and we ask for forgiveness in his name. **Amen.**

Prayer of Thanksgiving

God of grace and glory,
we give you thanks
that you have revealed your power and splendour
through your mighty acts of creation
and shown your redeeming and transforming love
through your belovèd Son.

We thank you for Jesus,
who lived and worked and suffered and died
for the sake of all the world,
and whom you raised from the dead
to be praised and exalted above all for ever.
We thank you that he died and was raised
to be Lord of the dead and the living,
so that, living or dying, we are his.
We thank you for the power of the Spirit,
at work in the world and the Church,
and for saints, apostles, prophets and martyrs,
who have testified to the gospel,
strengthened by grace, and sustained by faith, hope and love.

To you, immortal, invisible God, King of the ages,
with your Son and your Spirit,
be honour and glory for ever and ever. **Amen.**

Prayer of Dedication

Help us, O God,
to live, not for ourselves, but for you.
Inspire us, O God,
to take up the cross and follow Jesus.
Empower us, O God,
to obey your Spirit's promptings;
for we are yours eternally
in Jesus Christ our Lord. **Amen.**

SUNDAY BETWEEN 18 AND 24 SEPTEMBER

Twenty-fifth Sunday in Ordinary Time

Opening Sentence

Draw near to God, and he will draw near to you.

Prayer of Approach and Adoration

God, whose greatness is unsearchable,
whose glory is above the heavens,
from the rising of the sun to its setting,
your name is to be adored.
One generation praises your works to another
and declares your mighty acts.
Draw near to us in mercy,
as we approach you with faith,
and grant that we may worship you
with joy and gladness,
with reverence and awe,
to the glory of your name;
through Jesus Christ our Lord. **Amen.**

Prayer of Confession

Hear our prayer, compassionate God,
and forgive our many sins.
We confess that, blinded by our worldliness,
we have failed to see your glory;
deafened by our selfishness,
we have not heard the cry of the needy.
Forgive our bitter envy and our selfish ambition.
Forgive our pride and our arrogance,
our greed and our complacency.
Remake us in your image, we pray,
that we may live as you intend
and be worthy of the gospel of Christ.
We ask it for his sake. **Amen.**

Prayer of Thanksgiving

God of our salvation,
we thank you for creating the universe
and giving us a place within it.
We thank you for the joyful news
that you desire everyone to be saved
and to come to the knowledge of the truth.
We thank you that, to accomplish our salvation
and to teach us your truth,
you sent your only Son, Jesus Christ.
He is the one mediator between you and humankind,
who himself became human
and gave his life as a ransom for all.
We thank you for his dying and his rising
and his eternal reign in glory.
We thank you that he has shown us
that greatness lies in humble service,
and that the first must be the last
and the servant of all.
Grant that we may live out that teaching
in humility and generosity,
that in our lives, as in our prayers,
we may bless and praise your holy name;
through Jesus Christ our Lord. **Amen.**

Prayer of Dedication (based on a hymn by Charles Wesley)

Lord, we dedicate our lives to you.
Help us, trusting in you alone,
to do your will,
to fulfil our calling,
and to serve the present age;
through our Lord and Master Jesus Christ. **Amen.**

SUNDAY BETWEEN 25 SEPTEMBER AND 1 OCTOBER

Twenty-sixth Sunday in Ordinary Time

Opening Sentence

To the One who alone has immortality and dwells in unapproachable light, whom no one has ever seen or can see; to him be honour and eternal dominion. **Amen.**

Prayer of Approach and Adoration

Ever-living God,
before the blazing light of your glory
angels and archangels hide their faces.
Yet in your great compassion,
you have sent forth your light and truth into the world
in Jesus Christ, the Sun of Righteousness,
the Day-spring from on high.
Shine on us now, in our darkness, we pray,
and grant that, as we worship you,
we may catch a glimpse of your glory;
through him who is the Light of the World,
our Saviour Jesus Christ. **Amen.**

Prayer of Confession

'Repent and turn from your transgressions. Turn to God, and live.'

Father of mercies,
we confess to you and to one another
how far short we have fallen
of the pattern you have set before us
in your belovèd Son.
He emptied himself;
    we exalt ourselves.
He was humble;
    we are conceited.
He was generous;
    we are mean.
He was gracious;
    we are intolerant.

Have mercy upon us, loving God,
and help us to change our ways,
that we may pursue righteousness, godliness, faith,
love, endurance and gentleness,
fight the good fight of faith,
and take hold of the eternal life to which we have been called
in Jesus Christ our Lord. **Amen.**

Prayer of Thanksgiving

Generous God,
you richly provide for your children.
We thank you for your kindness.
You have given us the gift of life
and set us in a world of beauty.
Despite our base ingratitude
you have given us your Son,
who emptied himself of dazzling glory,
taking the form of a slave,
and was born in human likeness.
He humbled himself and became obedient to death –
even death on a cross.
Therefore you have highly exalted him
and given him the name above every name,
so that at the name of Jesus every knee should bend,
and every tongue confess that Jesus Christ is Lord,
to your glory, God our Father.
By the power of the Holy Spirit,
equip us to proclaim the good news of Christ,
and to praise you by our words and deeds;
through Jesus Christ our Lord. **Amen.**

Prayer of Dedication (based on a hymn by Charles Wesley)

Lord Jesus, to whom we all belong,
assert your sovereign right within our lives.
You justly claim us for your own
for you have bought us with a price.
Take our thankful songs and our loving hearts,
and use them for your glory;
for to you alone we live and we die.
We ask it in your name. **Amen.**

SUNDAY BETWEEN 2 AND 8 OCTOBER

Twenty-seventh Sunday in Ordinary Time

Opening Sentence

Grace, mercy and peace to you from God our Father and Christ Jesus our Lord.

Prayer of Adoration

'Be still before the Lord, and wait patiently for him.'

Let us in silence centre our minds on God.
Silence
How great is your being, eternal God;
how majestic is your name.
You hold all things in existence;
you are the fountain of life,
the source of all good,
the desire of our hearts
and the ground of our hope.
Without you we are nothing.
All praise and glory be yours alone,
for ever and ever. **Amen.**

Prayer of Confession

God of compassion and mercy,
you have taught us in your word
that the righteous live by faith.
Forgive us for misplacing our trust.
Forgive us for depending on our own understanding
and our own wisdom.
Forgive us for relying on our own good deeds,
and our own strength.
Help us to trust in you alone, and increase our faith
that we may guard the good treasure entrusted to us,
with the help of the indwelling Spirit,
and press on towards the goal that you have set before us
in Jesus Christ our Lord. **Amen.**

Prayer of Thanksgiving

The heavens declare your glory, O God,
and the earth redounds to your praise.
We thank you for the beauty and splendour of creation
and for the rich diversity of life within it.
We thank you for revealing yourself to the world
in many and various ways by the prophets
and by your eternal Son,
the heir of all things,
through whom you created the worlds.
Born of Mary, he lived among us,
proclaiming your kingdom
with words of truth and with signs and wonders.
We thank you for his dying and rising
by which he abolished death
and brought life and immortality to light.
We thank you for exalting him,
high above all angels and powers,
and for the gifts of the Holy Spirit,
distributed according to his will.
By the same Spirit,
graciously guide us on our journey
and bring us with all your saints
to the joy and peace of your kingdom;
through Jesus Christ our Lord. **Amen.**

Prayer of Dedication

In your grace and mercy,
God, our strength and hope,
instil in us a spirit of power,
of love and of self-discipline,
that the lives which we dedicate to you now
may bring forth fruit that is good,
to the praise of your wonderful name.
We ask it for the sake of your Son,
our Saviour Jesus Christ. **Amen.**

SUNDAY BETWEEN 9 AND 15 OCTOBER

Twenty-eighth Sunday in Ordinary Time

Opening Sentence

Great are the works of the Lord, whose righteousness endures for ever.

Prayer of Approach and Adoration

Most holy God,
glorious in power and resplendent in majesty,
who are we to come into your presence?
Yet through Christ Jesus, your dear Son,
who is our great high priest,
we approach your throne with boldness,
confident in the knowledge of your generous love,
your mercy and your grace.
We rejoice in you, most holy God,
and we praise you in Christ's name. **Amen.**

Prayer of Confession

God, to whom alone we owe allegiance,
we have not loved you as you deserve
or served our neighbours as you have commanded.
In mind and in heart we have been impure.
In word and in deed we have been unkind.
In negligence and ignorance
we have failed to act with righteousness
and to work for peace and justice.
Forgive our sins
and so fill our thoughts
with what is true and honourable,
just and pure,
pleasing and commendable,
excellent and praiseworthy,
that our words and actions may be worthy of our calling;
through Jesus Christ our Lord. **Amen.**

Prayer of Thanksgiving

We thank you, God eternal,
for creating and sustaining the universe
and for all the blessings you shower upon us.
You have done great and wonderful things,
plans formed of old, faithful and sure.
We thank you for the redemption of humankind
by our Lord Jesus Christ,
who has taken away the sin of the world.
By his death he has destroyed death,
and by his resurrection he has restored to us eternal life.
He is our great high priest,
able to sympathize with our weakness,
who pleads for us in heaven.
We thank you for the gift of the Holy Spirit,
who comes to work in our lives,
bringing salvation to us,
that we may die with Christ and rise with him.
We thank you for the Church
in which we are nurtured and nourished,
challenged and called
to show our love for you by our care for others
and our zeal to proclaim the gospel.
For these and all your innumerable blessings
we give you thanks and praise;
through Jesus Christ our Lord. **Amen.**

Prayer of Dedication

God, whose overflowing grace
has blessed us all our days,
we give ourselves again to you.
Use us for your kingdom's sake
and grant us that peace,
beyond our understanding,
which guards our hearts and minds
in Jesus Christ our Lord.
We ask it in his name. **Amen.**

SUNDAY BETWEEN 16 AND 22 OCTOBER

Twenty-ninth Sunday in Ordinary Time

Opening Sentences

Declare God's glory among the nations, his marvellous works among all the peoples. Honour and majesty are before him; strength and beauty are in his sanctuary.

Prayer of Adoration

God most high,
we worship you in your holy splendour
and bow our hearts before you.
You are the true and living God;
beside you there is no other.
You preserve our life;
you neither slumber nor sleep;
you are our refuge and our dwelling-place.
Majestic and glorious, merciful and loving,
you are worthy of all praise
now and in all eternity;
through Jesus Christ our Lord. **Amen.**

Prayer of Confession

God, our Shepherd,
we confess that we have wandered from your paths.
Like sheep we have gone astray;
we have turned to our own way.
We have lived as if we had no need of you.
We have shut you out of our lives.
We have done what is wrong
and failed to do what is right.
We have ignored the poor and helpless
and neglected to feed the hungry.
We have been quick to please ourselves
and slow to do your will.

For the sake of your Son, who died for us,
forgive our persistent sin;
and lead us in paths of righteousness.
We ask it in Christ's name. **Amen.**

Prayer of Thanksgiving

Incomparable God,
the universe is your creation
and we are your people,
fashioned and loved by you.
When we strayed from your paths,
you sent your dear Son
to rescue us from selfishness and pride.
He came, not to be served, but to serve
and to give his life to ransom many.
Oppressed and afflicted, wounded and crushed,
he died on the Cross,
displaying the victory of self-giving love.
Raised again by your mighty power,
he reigns in glory and loves us still,
and it is he who will judge the living and the dead.
We thank you for the message of the gospel,
coming to us in the power of the Spirit,
and we pray that, in the Spirit's strength,
we may be proficient and equipped for every good work
to carry out the ministry which you have entrusted to us.
And to you, with your Son and your Spirit,
be all honour and blessing for ever. **Amen.**

Prayer of Dedication

God of our salvation,
all life belongs to you.
Your Son has broken down the barrier
between sacred and secular,
between spiritual and material,
between heaven and earth.
So we offer you every part of our lives
to be used to your glory and praise;
through Jesus Christ our Lord. **Amen.**

SUNDAY BETWEEN 23 AND 29 OCTOBER

Thirtieth Sunday in Ordinary Time

Opening Sentence

Happy are those whose strength is in the Lord of hosts.

Prayer of Adoration

To you, O God, be glory for ever.
Holy is your name.
You dwell in majesty and might.
Holy is your name.
You act with truth and righteousness.
Holy is your name.
You love the world without reserve.
Holy is your name.
You deal with us with great compassion.
Holy is your name.
To you, O God, be glory for ever.
Holy is your name. Amen.

Prayer of Confession

Holy God,
you call us to a life of holiness
and command us to love you with our whole being
and our neighbours as ourselves.
We confess that we have disobeyed your call
and broken your commandments.
We have sought to please others
and failed to please you.
We have yielded to temptation
and turned from your ways.
We have gratified our own desires
and ignored the needs of our neighbours.
We have been selfish and greedy
and reluctant to share with others.
We have been proud and complacent
and unready for humble service.

In mercy and grace, forgive us,
and plant in our hearts such love for you and our neighbours
that our lives shall show forth your praise;
through Jesus Christ our Lord. **Amen.**

Prayer of Thanksgiving

Great are the things you have done for us,
God of extravagant love.
We thank you for the world in which we live,
for its beauty and variety,
and for the goodness of your creation.
We thank you for your love for the world,
revealed in Jesus your Son,
who for us became human
and taught us how we should live.
We thank you that in your kingdom the humble are exalted
and that greatness is found in self-giving service.
We thank you that Jesus offered himself
once for all upon the Cross;
and that, risen from death, he is exalted above the heavens,
our high priest, holy, blameless and undefiled,
who lives for ever to make intercession for us.
We thank you that the Holy Spirit,
sent in the name of Christ,
has gathered us into the Church,
to worship and serve you with sisters and brothers
from every part of the earth.
We thank you for the glorious hope of life immortal,
promised to us in Christ,
and we pray that you will keep us loyal,
to fight the good fight, finish the race,
keep the faith, and win the crown of righteousness;
through Jesus Christ our Lord. **Amen.**

Prayer of Dedication (based on a hymn by Charles Wesley)

Lord Jesus, to whom alone we owe allegiance,
we are no longer our own, but yours.
We joyfully dedicate our souls and bodies
to your glory, now and in all eternity. **Amen.**

ALL SAINTS

Opening Sentences

Blessed are the poor in spirit, for theirs is the kingdom of heaven.
Blessed are the pure in heart, for they will see God.

Prayer of Adoration

With all your people, on earth and in heaven,
we praise your name, O God,
for you alone are worthy of adoration.
Majestic and glorious, encircled in light,
radiant in splendour, stupendous in love,
rich in mercy, abounding in grace,
you reign supreme beyond space and time.
In you is the fullness of perfection;
in you is our hope of salvation;
in you is the promise of life eternal.
With all your people, on earth and in heaven,
we praise your name, O God;
through Jesus Christ our Lord. **Amen.**

Prayer of Confession

Forgive us, God of mercy,
for our narrow and limited vision
and our reluctance to trust in what we cannot see.
Forgive our preoccupation with the here and now
and our failure to seek the things above.
Forgive our earthbound thinking
and our feeble sense of the communion of saints.
Rekindle in us, by your Holy Spirit,
the sacred fire of your love
and remind us of the things eternal,
that with clean hands and pure hearts
we may serve you faithfully on earth
and come at last, with all your saints,
to the peace and joy of heaven;
through Jesus Christ our Lord. **Amen.**

Prayer of Thanksgiving

Blessing and glory, thanksgiving and honour
be to our God for ever and ever.

The earth is the Lord's, and all that is in it;
the world, and all its inhabitants.
Blessing and glory, thanksgiving and honour
be to our God for ever and ever.

Salvation belongs to our God, who is seated on the throne,
and to the Lamb, who has taken away the world's sin.
Blessing and glory, thanksgiving and honour
be to our God for ever and ever.

God has shown his love for us by sending his only Son,
who lived and died and rose again, that we might have eternal life.
Blessing and glory, thanksgiving and honour
be to our God for ever and ever.

The souls of the righteous are safe in God's hands.
They are at peace; they abide in his love.
Blessing and glory, thanksgiving and honour
be to our God for ever and ever.

See what love the Father has given us, that we should be called his children.
The holy ones of the Most High shall possess the kingdom for ever.
Blessing and glory, thanksgiving and honour
be to our God for ever and ever. Amen.

Prayer of Dedication

Eternal God,
receive the lives which we offer to you,
and bring us at last
to join that great multitude,
from all nations and peoples and languages,
which stands before your throne and worships you
in never-ending praise;
through Jesus Christ our Lord. **Amen.**

SUNDAY BETWEEN 30 OCTOBER AND 5 NOVEMBER

Thirty-first Sunday in Ordinary Time

Opening Sentences

Send out your light and your truth, O God; let them lead me. Let them bring me to your holy hill. Then will I go to the altar of God, my exceeding joy; and I will praise you, O God my God.

Prayer of Adoration

Glory be to you, God the Father,
resplendent in majesty and might,
maker of all and shepherd of your people.
Glory be to God,
glory and praise for ever.

Glory be to you, God the Son,
eternal Word of the Father,
redeemer of all and saviour of your people.
Glory be to God,
glory and praise for ever.

Glory be to you, God the Spirit,
fountain of light and giver of life,
sustainer of all and advocate of your people.
Glory be to God,
glory and praise for ever.

Glory be to you, God the Father,
Glory be to you, God the Son,
Glory be to you, God the Spirit,
Glory be to you, most holy Trinity,
Glory be to God,
glory and praise for ever. Amen.

Prayer of Confession

Happy are they, whose way is blameless,
who walk in your ways, O God,
and keep your decrees.

We confess that we are not among them.
We have sinned against you exceedingly,
and against our sisters and brothers.
We have broken your commandments,
and failed to care for others.
Wash us, and make us clean,
that, ceasing to do evil and learning to do good,
we may seek justice and defend the oppressed,
and the name of Jesus may be glorified in us.
We ask it for his sake. **Amen.**

Prayer of Thanksgiving

Living God,
whose love for your creation knows no limit,
we praise you for your grace and mercy.
You sent your Son to seek and save the lost.
He welcomed penitent sinners and those whom others despised.
He obtained eternal redemption,
offering himself to you without blemish, through the eternal Spirit,
so that, though our sins are like scarlet, they shall become like snow,
and drawing us into your kingdom of righteousness, joy and peace.
We bless you for new life which you give us in Christ
and we pray that we may be filled with power,
with your Spirit, and with justice and might,
to declare your wonderful acts
and lead lives worthy of you,
who have called us into your kingdom and glory;
through Jesus Christ our Lord. **Amen.**

Prayer of Dedication (based on a hymn by Charles Wesley)

Lord Jesus Christ, our Saviour from sin,
you died that we might live,
no longer for ourselves but for you,
and give ourselves without reserve
to you who gave yourself for us.
Take us for your own,
and so change and purify us
that your glorious name may be honoured in us,
now and for ever. **Amen.**

SUNDAY BETWEEN 6 AND 12 NOVEMBER

Thirty-second Sunday in Ordinary Time

Opening Sentences

Let all who seek God rejoice and be glad in him. Let those who love his salvation say evermore, 'God is great.'

Prayer of Approach and Adoration

God of wisdom, radiant and unfading,
the Saviour of those who seek refuge in you,
you are our help and deliverer,
you comfort the hearts of the afflicted.
In our weakness and weariness
we come into your gracious presence.
Receive the worship we offer,
unworthy as it is,
and by the power of the Holy Spirit
equip us to do your will
to the glory of your holy name;
through Jesus Christ our Lord. **Amen.**

Prayer of Confession

Maker and Judge of all,
it is your will that justice should roll down like waters
and righteousness like an overflowing stream.
We confess our share in the human sin
that leads to injustice and wickedness.
We confess our pride and aggression,
our covetousness and greed.
We confess our intolerance and prejudice,
our apathy and indolence.
We confess our unkindness and meanness,
our complacency and self-righteousness.
We repent of all our sins
and ask you to forgive us.
Wondrously show your steadfast love

and turn our hearts from sin to you
that we may work for righteousness and justice
and bring you glory and honour;
for the sake of Jesus Christ our Lord. **Amen.**

Prayer of Thanksgiving

We thank you, living God,
for the knowledge we have of you,
in your splendour and might,
in your grace and truth,
in your mercy and love.
We thank you for the revelation you have given us
in Jesus Christ your Son,
and for the life eternal which you promise us in him.
He lived on earth, and died on the Cross
and you raised him to life, the firstborn of the dead.
We know that our Redeemer lives for ever
and believe that, as he died and rose again,
you will bring to life with him
those who have died in the faith of Christ.
By the power of your gracious Spirit,
help us always to stand firm in that faith,
to hold fast to the truths of the gospel,
to proclaim them in word and deed,
and to come, with all your people,
to your glorious, eternal kingdom;
through Jesus Christ our Lord. **Amen.**

Prayer of Dedication

Living Father, God of peace,
we give our lives to you.
Living Saviour, Jesus Christ,
we give our lives to you.
Living Advocate, Holy Spirit,
we give our lives to you.
Father, Son and Holy Spirit,
we give our lives to you. Amen.

SUNDAY BETWEEN 13 AND 19 NOVEMBER

Thirty-third Sunday in Ordinary Time

Opening Sentence

Make a joyful noise to the Lord, all the earth; break forth into joyous song and sing praises.

Prayer of Adoration

Eternal God,
you have been our dwelling-place in all generations.
Before the mountains were brought forth,
before you had formed the earth,
from everlasting to everlasting you are God.
A thousand years in your sight are like a day that is past
or like a watch in the night.
Your wisdom and knowledge are limitless;
your goodness and mercy are without end.
All glory and praise belong to you, now and in all eternity;
through Jesus Christ our Lord. **Amen.**

Prayer of Confession

God, most holy and most merciful,
we confess our many sins to you and ask you to forgive us.
You have given us bountiful gifts but we have taken them for granted.
You have given us the gift of time,
but we have squandered and wasted it.
You have given us the capacity to reason
but we have been lazy in using our minds.
You have given us skills and talents
but we have not used them for your glory or the benefit of others.
You have given us families, friends and neighbours
but we have not cared for them as we should.
In your tender kindness, forgive us and restore us,
that we may use your gifts aright to your glory and praise,
in the strength of your Holy Spirit,
and the grace of our Lord Jesus Christ,
in whose name we pray. **Amen.**

Prayer of Thanksgiving

Let us give our thanks to God, as we reflect on his wonderful works.

Let us thank God for creation;
for in his mind the galaxies were conceived,
and by his will the universe was formed.
Silence
We thank you, O God, for you are good;
your love endures for ever.

Let us thank God for his redeeming work;
for he destined us for salvation
through Jesus Christ, who died for us,
and was raised again,
so that, living or dying, we might be with him.
Silence
We thank you, O God, for you are good;
your love endures for ever.

Let us thank God for the Spirit;
for he is at work in the world
and in the Church, the Body of Christ,
empowering us for mission and service.
Silence
We thank you, O God, for you are good;
your love endures for ever.

Let us thank God for the faithful departed;
for by his grace they fought the good fight of faith,
remaining constant in the face of persecution and hardship,
and they inspire us by their example.
Silence
We thank you, O God, for you are good;
your love endures for ever. Amen.

Prayer of Dedication

As we offer our gifts to you, O God,
we pray that our lives may be to your praise.
Help us not to grow weary in doing what is right,
and enable us to encourage one another,
and all the more as we see your great Day approaching;
through Jesus Christ our Lord. **Amen.**

SUNDAY BETWEEN 20 AND 26 NOVEMBER

Sunday before Advent

Opening Sentence

Grace to you and peace from him who is and who was and who is to come.

Prayer of Approach and Adoration

God, the rock of our salvation,
we come into your presence with songs of praise,
for you are a great and mighty God.
In your hand are the depths of the earth
and the mountain heights are yours too.
The sea is yours, for you made it,
and the dry land, formed by your hands.
And we are yours,
created by your love and sustained by your goodness.
We worship and adore you, our Maker and our God;
in the name of Jesus Christ our Lord. **Amen.**

Prayer of Confession

God, the Shepherd of your people,
we confess that we have gone astray.

We confess that we have disobeyed your call
and broken your commandments.
We have not sought your guidance but have followed our own paths.
Silence
In your grace and mercy,
pardon and restore us.

We confess that we have not served Christ by serving our neighbours.
We have not fed the hungry, clothed the naked,
cared for the sick or welcomed the stranger.
Silence
In your grace and mercy,
pardon and restore us.

Here is good news for all who repent.
Jesus says: 'Your sins are forgiven.'
Thanks be to God. **Amen.**

Prayer of Thanksgiving

Gracious God,
we thank you for your overflowing love.
You seek those who have gone astray, bind up the injured,
and strengthen those who are weak.
To bring lost sinners back to you
you gave your only Son,
in whom all things were made.
He came to proclaim a kingdom
that was not of this world –
your kingdom of justice, mercy and grace.
He suffered and died
and you raised him to life,
the firstborn of all creation,
and the firstborn of the dead,
offering to all new life in him.
He is exalted and glorious in heaven
and to him you have given authority and glory,
an everlasting dominion that shall never end.
Through the life-giving Spirit
you inspire and empower the Church
to proclaim the kingdom and serve the world.
We rejoice, gracious God, in your mighty acts,
and give you our praise and thanks;
through Jesus Christ our Lord. **Amen.**

Prayer of Dedication (based on a hymn by Charles Wesley)

Lord Jesus, the friend of sinners,
the Shepherd who died for the sheep,
into your blessèd hands
receive our talents, gifts and graces.
Enlarge and fill our hearts
with your own boundless love,
and let us live to proclaim your word,
that our lives may be to your glory,
now and for ever. **Amen.**

CHURCH ANNIVERSARY

Opening Sentence

God is spirit, and those who worship him must worship in spirit and in truth.

Prayer of Approach and Adoration

God, changeless and true,
you keep your covenant
and show steadfast love to your servants.
You are the God of our ancestors,
faithful in each generation.
Heaven and the highest heaven cannot contain you;
how much less this house that we have built.
And yet to us, as we gather here,
this is indeed your house and the gate of heaven.
Help us to worship you
with reverent wonder,
with joyous praise,
in spirit and in truth;
through Jesus Christ our Lord. **Amen.**

Prayer of Confession

Let us confess our sins, and ask God to forgive us.

Our ingratitude for all you have done for us,
God of mercy, forgive.
Our failure to pray and study your word,
God of mercy, forgive.
Our lack of preparation for worship,
God of mercy, forgive.
Our scant concern for peace and unity,
God of mercy, forgive.
Our reluctance to proclaim the gospel,
God of mercy, forgive.
Our slowness to reach out in service,
God of mercy, forgive.

We hear Christ's word of grace: Your sins are forgiven.
Thanks be to God. **Amen.**

Prayer of Thanksgiving

Ever-living God,
we give you thanks
that you made the world to resound to your praise.
You created human beings in your image and likeness
and gave us creative vision and inventive skill.
We thank you that, to restore what human sin had spoilt,
you sent to us your Son Jesus Christ.
He lived among us, and we saw his glory.
He defeated death by dying for us.
He was raised from the dead and exalted to heaven.
We thank you that through him you sent your Holy Spirit
to make us citizens with the saints
and members of your household,
built on the foundation of the apostles and prophets,
with Jesus Christ as the chief cornerstone.
You call us to be a royal priesthood
offering spiritual sacrifices to you and proclaiming your mighty acts.
We thank you that this house of prayer
has been built to your glory,
to help us on our way to the heavenly city, the new Jerusalem,
where Christ will give his light for ever.
We thank you for the fellowship
of those who have worshipped in this place,
and we pray that all who seek you here may find you,
and, being filled with the Holy Spirit,
may become a living temple,
a dwelling-place for your life-giving presence in the world.
We ask it through Jesus Christ our Lord. **Amen.**

Prayer of Dedication

Generous God,
to whose glory we celebrate the anniversary of this church,
we thank you for the faithful witness
of those who have served you here.
By the power of the Holy Spirit,
make us faithful in our generation
as we offer our lives in your service;
through Jesus Christ our Lord. **Amen.**

HARVEST THANKSGIVING

Opening Sentence

As long as the earth endures, says God, seedtime and harvest, cold and heat, summer and winter, day and night, shall not cease.

Prayer of Adoration

Glory and honour are yours by right,
God of power and God of grace,
for you created all things, and by your will they exist.
We praise you, mighty creator,
whose glory is reflected in what you have made.
How perfect you are in power and wisdom!
How beautiful, how good is your creation!
Still more we praise you, gracious God,
because you have revealed yourself to us,
not only in the world about us,
but in the person of your Son,
in whom we see the majesty and splendour
of your redeeming love.
God of power and God of grace,
we worship and adore you;
through Jesus Christ our Lord. **Amen.**

Prayer of Confession

Sovereign God,
you are our maker, to whom we owe our every breath,
and you have set us in a world of beauty.
We do not deserve your love.
We confess with shame
that we have been unfaithful creatures,
unworthy stewards of creation.
We have taken your generous gifts for granted
and squandered and polluted them.
Forgive us, we pray, our ingratitude,
our complacency and our pride.
Pardon our selfishness,
our abuse and misuse of your bounty.

Grant that, with thankful hearts,
we may use your gifts aright,
and share what we have, by your mercy,
with all who need our help;
for the sake of Jesus Christ our Lord. **Amen.**

Prayer of Thanksgiving

We thank you, God most generous,
for the splendour and beauty of creation,
for the ordered succession of seasons,
for your love which made it all.
We thank you for the good and fertile earth,
for the fruits of the earth in their seasons,
for the life that sustains our life, for the food that we daily enjoy.
We thank you for those whose labour supplies our physical needs –
for those who harvest crops, those who transport them,
those who process them, those who sell them.

We thank you, God most generous,
for your most wonderful gift – Jesus, our Saviour and Lord,
for his living and dying and rising,
for the redemption of the world in him.
We thank you for the Holy Spirit, the Lord and the giver of life,
for the Church, your new creation,
and for the privilege which is ours of belonging to Christ's body.

We thank you, God most generous, whose mercies endure for ever;
through Jesus Christ our Lord. **Amen.**

Prayer of Dedication

God of love,
as we thank you for your marvellous acts
in the creation and redemption of the world,
we offer ourselves to you in gratitude,
that we may serve you
and our sisters and brothers
joyfully and faithfully throughout our lives;
in the name of Jesus Christ our Lord. **Amen.**

JOHN AND CHARLES WESLEY

Opening Sentence

Sing praises to the Lord, for he has done gloriously; let this be known in all the earth.

Prayer of Approach and Adoration

Glory be to you, God the Father,
for you have found a way for the recovery of lost sinners.
Glory be to you, God the Son,
for you have loved us and washed us from our sins.
Glory be to you, God the Holy Spirit,
for you have given us life and freedom.
God the Father, God the Son and God the Holy Spirit,
to you be glory and blessing and honour and might
for ever and ever. **Amen.**

Prayer of Confession

God of truth and love,
we confess with shame that we have sinned against you
and against one another.
We have not loved you
with all our heart and soul and mind and strength.
We have not loved our neighbours as ourselves.
We have neglected the means of grace.
We have been insincere and thoughtless in worship.
We have turned our backs on those in need.
We have been selfish and intolerant.
But, while we were still helpless,
Christ died for the ungodly;
and we trust in Christ, Christ alone, for salvation.
Grant to us, we pray,
the assurance that Christ has taken away our sins
and saved us from the law of sin and death.
We ask it in his name. **Amen.**

Prayer of Thanksgiving

Eternal God, maker of heaven and earth,
eternal God our Father,
as we thank you for creating us in your image,
so we praise you still more for sending your Son
to restore what we had lost.
We thank you for his lowly birth, his precious passion,
his mighty resurrection and his glorious ascension.
We praise you that he has gone to prepare a place for us,
that where he is, we may also ascend
and reign with him in glory.
We thank you for sending to us the Holy Spirit,
who enables us to call you Father.
We bless you that in every age
you have raised up faithful witnesses to your truth,
and at this time we thank you especially
for all that you accomplished through John and Charles Wesley,
who brought many to accept your precious and very great promise
that they might become participants in your divine nature.
Grant to us such a warming of our hearts
that we, being set afire by holy love,
may spread its flame to the uttermost parts of the earth;
through Jesus Christ our Lord. **Amen.**

Prayer of Dedication (based on a hymn by Charles Wesley)

God of all-redeeming grace,
by whose hands we were created
and set free from sin,
we thank you for all your gifts to us.
As we offer this our sacrifice of praise,
we lay before you all we have and all we are
that we may be used to your glory here on earth,
until we are gathered to the Church above
and sing the songs of heaven.
We pray in the name of Jesus Christ our Lord. **Amen.**

NEW YEAR: WATCHNIGHT

Opening Sentence

God says: I am the Alpha and the Omega, the beginning and the end.

Prayer of Approach and Adoration

Ever-living God, the beginning and the end,
how majestic is your name in all the earth!
From everlasting to everlasting you are God.
A thousand years in your sight are like a day that is past
or like a watch in the night.
You are beyond all time and space.
You will still be when heaven and earth have passed away.
Into your timeless presence we come as a new year dawns.
Accept our worship, we pray,
and help us to see the passing of time in the light of your eternity;
through Jesus Christ our Lord. **Amen.**

Prayer of Confession

God of our salvation,
as one year ends and another begins,
we confess our sins to you.

We confess that we have been
  half-hearted in worship,
  inconstant in prayer,
  slow to obey you,
  deaf to your call.
We confess that we have been
  selfish and slothful,
  greedy and envious,
  quick to condemn
  and slow to forgive.

In your great mercy,
forgive us and heal us;
and strengthen our resolve,
in the power of the Spirit,
to love and serve you and our neighbours,

to the glory of your name;
through Jesus Christ our Lord. **Amen.**

Prayer of Thanksgiving

Immortal God,
we give you thanks
that in your providence you have brought us safely
to the end of another year.
We thank you for the blessings we have received
   through the beauty of nature
   and the changing seasons,
   through art and music,
   through prose and poetry,
   through those who love us
   and those we have sought to help.
We thank you for our Lord Jesus Christ,
   living and dying and rising,
   reigning for ever in glory,
   constantly praying for us,
   as we continue on our journey.
We thank you for the Holy Spirit,
   indwelling and inspiring,
   strengthening and challenging,
   leading us to heaven.
Your goodness and mercy have followed us all the days of our life.
Grant that we may enter this new year,
trusting in your unfailing love,
and serve you with grateful and obedient hearts;
through Jesus Christ our Lord. **Amen.**

Prayer of Dedication (based on a hymn by Charles Wesley)

Gracious God,
we are thankful for all your past mercies
and your continued care for us.
Through your Son
we offer ourselves to you.
Our residue of days or hours
shall be yours, wholly yours,
a living sacrifice of praise to you;
through Jesus Christ our Lord. **Amen.**

REMEMBRANCE SUNDAY

Opening Sentence

God is our refuge and strength, a very present help in trouble.

Prayer of Approach and Adoration

God of love,
you make the sun rise and the rain fall
on the good and the evil alike.
You show no partiality;
you have no favourites.
You are a stronghold for the oppressed;
you do not overlook
the cry of the afflicted.
We worship and adore you.
May we sense your healing presence
on this day of remembrance;
and may we know your reconciling love,
now and always;
through the merits of Jesus Christ our Saviour. **Amen.**

Prayer of Confession

Forgive us, God of compassion,
for our share in the sin of the world.
Your Son our Saviour taught us
that we should love our enemies.
We confess that hatred and hostility
have often driven out love.
Your Son our Saviour taught us
to love one another as he loved us.
We confess that selfishness and pride
have often driven out love.
Forgive our failure to do good,
our compromise with evil,
our feeble efforts for justice and peace,
and our hard, unmerciful hearts.
Grant us such awareness of your limitless grace
that we may be agents of your reconciling love;
through Jesus Christ our Lord. **Amen.**

Prayer of Thanksgiving

We give you thanks and praise,
most merciful living God,
for the world which you have created
and given into our care.
We thank you for your faithfulness,
despite our constant sin,
and for sending Jesus Christ your Son
to reconcile us to you.
We thank you for his life of love,
his passion and death upon the Cross,
his glorious resurrection and exaltation
and the gift of the Spirit, sent in his name.
We thank you for all who, living and dying,
have given themselves in love and service;
and we thank you that nothing in all creation
can separate us from your love in Jesus Christ our Lord.
We thank you for the vision of a world
where swords are beaten into ploughshares
and spears into pruning hooks.
Inspire us by your Spirit to work towards that goal
and bring us, in your mercy, to the heavenly city
where you will swallow up death for ever
and wipe away the tears from every face.
We ask it for the sake of Jesus Christ our Saviour. **Amen.**

Prayer of Dedication

God of all grace,
you call your children
to live as sisters and brothers
and have given your Son to be our Saviour,
the Prince of Peace.
As we yield our lives to your service,
grant that we, who are called by his name,
may strive for understanding, reconciliation and peace,
and live to your praise and glory;
through Jesus Christ our Lord. **Amen.**